Worship as a Lifestyle
A Core Course of the School of Leadership

Church of the Nazarene
Mesoamerica Region

Timothy Mckeithen

Worship as a Lifestyle

A book in the "School of Leadership" series.
Core Level Course

Autor: Timothy Mckeithen
Co-Autores: Luisa Zickefoose
　　　　　　Franlyn Peña Ortiz

Spanish Editor: Dr. Mónica E. Mastronardi de Fernández
Spanish Reviewer: Dr. Rubén Fernández
Translators: Dr. Stephen J. Bennett, Rev. Dr. Veora L Tressler, Tamara Zambrana.
Reviewer: Shelley J. Webb

Material produced by EDUCATION AND CLERGY DEVELOPMENT
of the Church of the Nazarene, Mesoamerica Region. www.edunaz.org
Mailing Address: PO Box 3977 - 1000 San José, Costa Rica, Central América.
Phone (506) 2285-0432 / 0423 - Email: EL@mesoamericaregion.org

Publisher and Distributor: Asociación Región Mesoamérica
Av. 12 de Octubre Plaza Victoria Locales 5 y 6
Pueblo Nuevo Hato Pintado, Ciudad de Panamá
Tel. (507) 203-3541
E-mail: literatura@mesoamericaregion.org

Copyright © 2017 - All rights reserved.
Reproduction whole or in part, by any means, without written permission from
Education and Clergy Development of the Church of the Nazarene, Mesoamerica Region is prohibited.
www.mesoamericaregion.org

All Biblical quotations are from the New International Version-2011, unless otherwise noted.

Design: Juan Manuel Fernandez (www.juanfernandez.ga)
Cover image: KOREphotos
Cover images and interiors of the covers used with permission under license by Creative Commons.

Digital printing

Table of Contents

Lesson 1	What is Worship?	9
Lesson 2	Worship in the Old Testament	17
Lesson 3	Worship in the New Testament	25
Lesson 4	Worship as a Lifestyle	33
Lesson 5	Congregational Worship	41
Lesson 6	The Holy Spirit and Worship	49
Lesson 7	Stewardship as an Act of Worship	57
Lesson 8	Cultural Fundamentals of Worship	65

Introduction

The book series **School of Leadership** is designed with the purpose of providing a tool to the church for formation, education and training of its members to actively integrate into Christian service the gifts and calling (vocation) they have received from the Lord.

Each book provides study materials for one course in the **School of Leadership** program offered by the theological Institutions of the Mesoamerica Region of the Church of the Nazarene. These institutions include: IBN (Coban, Guatemala); STN (Guatemala City); SENAMEX (Mexico City); SENDAS (San Jose, Costa Rica); SND (Santo Domingo, Dominican Republic); and SETENAC (Havana, Cuba). A number of leaders from these schools (presidents, directors, vice presidents and directors of decentralized academic studies) actively participated in the program design.

The **School of Leadership** has five core courses that are common to all ministries, and six specialized courses for each ministry area, at the end of which, the respective theological institution awards the student a certificate (or diploma) in Specialized Ministry.

The overall objective of the **School of Leadership** is "to work with the local church in equipping the saints for the work of the ministry establishing a solid biblical and theological foundation and developing them through the practice of exercising their gifts for service in the local congregation and society as a whole." The specific objectives of this program are threefold:

- Develop the ministerial gifts of the local congregation.
- Multiply service ministries in the church and community.
- Raise awareness of the vocation of professional ministry in its diverse forms.

We thank Dr. Monica Mastronardi de Fernandez for her dedication as General Editor of the project, and the Regional Coordinators of Ministries and the team of writers and designers who collaborated to publish these books. We are equally grateful to the teachers who will share these materials. They will make a difference in the lives of thousands of people in the Mesoamerica Region and beyond.

Finally, we thank Dr. L. Carlos Saenz, Mesoamerica Regional Director, for his continued support in this work, which is the result of his conviction that the church must be holistically equipped.

We pray for God's blessing for all the disciples whose lives and Christian service will be enriched by these books.

Dr. Ruben E. Fernandez
Theological Education Coordinator
Mesoamerica Region

What Is the School of Leadership?

The School of Leadership is an educational program for lay ministry in different specialties to engage in the mission of the local church. This program is administered by the Theological Institutions of the Church of the Nazarene in the Mesoamerica Region and taught both at these institutions and in the local churches enrolled in the program.

Who Can Benefit from the School of Leadership?

It is for all the members of the Church of the Nazarene who have participated in Levels B and C of the discipleship program, and who, with all their heart, wish to discover their gifts and serve God in His work.

The Plan ABCDE

In order to contribute to the formation of the members of their churches, the Church of the Nazarene in the Mesoamerica Region has adopted the plan of discipleship ABCDE, and since 2001 began publishing materials for each of these levels. The School of Leadership is Level D of the ABCDE discipleship plan and is designed for those who have been through previous levels of discipleship.

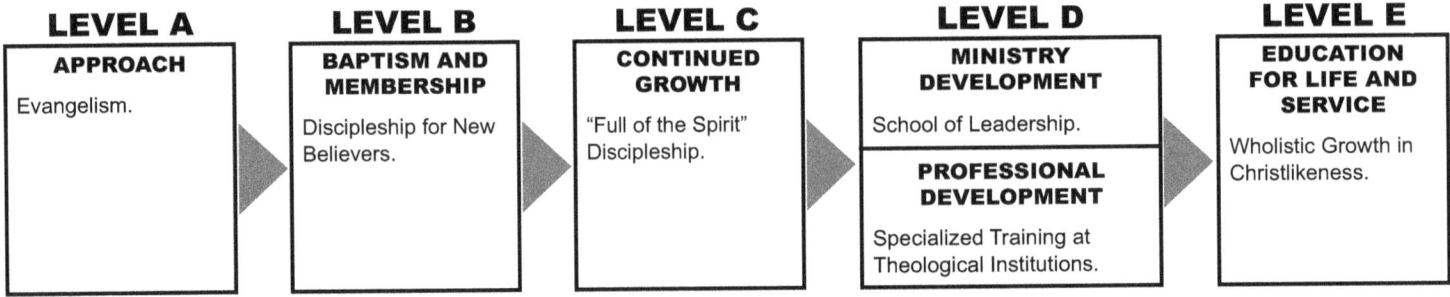

In the Church of the Nazarene, we believe making disciples in the image of Christ in the nations is the foundation of missionary work and the responsibility of leadership (Ephesians 4: 7-16). The work of discipleship is continuous and dynamic; therefore, the disciple never stops growing in the likeness of his Lord. This growth, when healthy, occurs in all dimensions: the individual dimension (spiritual growth), the corporate dimension (joining the congregation), the holiness in life dimension (progressive transformation of our being and doing according to the model of Jesus Christ) and the service dimension (investing our lives in ministry).

Dr. Monica Mastronardi de Fernandez
Managing Editor, The School of Leadership Book Series

How Do I Use This Book?

This book contains eight lessons of the School of Leadership program, along with activities and final evaluation of the course.

How are the contents of this book organized?

Each of the eight lessons of this book contains the following:

➢ **Objectives:** These are the learning objectives the student is expected to understand at the end of the lesson.

➢ **Main Ideas:** A summary of the key teachings of the lesson.

➢ **Development of Lesson:** This is the largest section because it is the development of the contents of the lesson. The lessons have been written so that the book can be the teacher, and for that reason the contents have been written in a dynamic form and in simple language with contemporary ideas.

➢ **Notes and Comments:** The information in the margins is intended to clarify terms and provide notes that complement or extend the content of the lesson.

➢ **Questions:** Sometimes questions are included in the margin that the teacher can use to introduce or reinforce a lesson topic.

➢ **What did we learn?:** The box at the end of the lesson development section provides a brief summary of the lesson.

➢ **Activities:** This is a page at the end of each lesson that contains learning activities, for individuals or groups, on the subject studied. The estimated time for implementation in class is 20 minutes.

➢ **Final evaluation of the course:** This is the last page of the book and once completed the student must remove it from the book and hand it in to a course instructor. The final evaluation should take about 15 minutes.

How long is each course?

The courses are designed for 12 hours of class over 8 ninety-minute sessions. Each institution and each church or local theological study center will coordinate days and times of the classes. Within this hour and a half the teacher or the teachers should include time for the activities contained in the book.

What is the role of the student?

The student is responsible for the following:

1. Enroll on time for the course.
2. Buy the book and study each lesson before class time.
3. Arrive for class on time.
4. Participate in class activities.
5. Participate in practical ministry in the local church outside of class.
6. Complete and submit the final evaluation to the teacher.

What is the role of the teacher of the course?

The professors and teachers for the School of Leadership courses are pastors and laity committed to the mission and ministry of the church and preferably have experience in the ministry they teach. The Director and/or the School of Leadership at the local church (or theological institution) invites their participation and their functions are the following:

1. Be well prepared by studying the book's content and scheduling the use of class time. When studying the lesson, you should have on hand the Bible and a dictionary. Although the lessons are written using simple language, it is recommended that you "translate" what you consider difficult in order to help the students understand. In other words, use terms that they can better understand.

2. Ensure that the students are studying the material in the book and achieving the learning objectives.

3. Plan and accompany students in the activities of ministerial practice. The local pastor and the director of the respective ministry must schedule these activities. These activities should not take away from class time.

4. Take daily attendance and grades in the class report form. The final average will be the result demonstrated by the student in the following activities:

   a. Class work
   b. Participation in ministerial practice outside of class
   c. Final evaluation

5. At the end of the course, collect the evaluation sheets and hand them in with the form "Class Report" to the local School of Leadership director. Do this after totaling the averages and verifying that all data is complete on the form.

6. Professors and teachers should not add tasks or reading assignments apart from the contents of the book. They should be creative in the design of the learning activities and in planning ministry activities outside the classroom according to the reality of their local church and its context.

How do I teach a class?

We recommend using a 90-minute class session as follows:

- **5 minutes:** Review the topic of the previous lesson and pray together.

- **30 minutes:** Review and discuss the lesson. We recommend using an outline, chalkboard, cardboard or other available materials, using dynamic learning activities and visual media such as graphics, drawings, objects, pictures, questions, assigning students to submit parts of the lesson, and so on. We do not recommend lecturing or having the teacher reread the lesson content.

- **5 minutes:** Break either in the middle of class or when it is convenient.

- **20 minutes:** Work on activities in the book. This can be done at the beginning, middle or end of the review, or you can complete the activities as you proceed in accordance with the issues as it relates to them.

• **20 minutes:** Discussion about the students' ministry practice that they currently do and that they will do. At the beginning of the course you will need to present the schedule to the students so that they can make arrangements to attend the ministry practice. In the classes when the students discuss their ministry practice, the conversation should be focused on what they learned, including their successes and their errors, as well as the difficulties they encountered.

• **10 minutes:** Prayer for the issues arising from the practice (challenges, people, problems, goals, gratitude for the results, among others).

How do I implement the final course evaluation?

Allocate 15 minutes of time during the last class meeting for the course evaluation. If necessary, students may consult their books and Bibles. Final evaluations are designed to be an activity to reinforce what was learned in class and not a repetition of the contents of the book. The purpose of this assessment is to measure the understanding and evaluation of the student concerning the class topics, their spiritual growth, their progress in the commitment to the mission of the church and their progress in ministerial experience.

Ministerial Practice Activities

The following are suggested activities for ministerial practice outside of class. The list below includes several ideas to help teachers, pastors, directors of local School of Leadership groups and local ministry directors. From the list you can choose the practice most suited to the contextual situation and the local church ministry, or others can replace these according to the needs and possibilities of your context.

We recommend having at least three ministerial activities per course. You can put the whole class to work on a project or assign group tasks according to interests, gifts and abilities. It is advisable to involve students in a variety of new ministry experiences.

Suggested Practical Ministry Activities
Worship as a Lifestyle

1. Have the students form committees to organize a worship service with emphasis on Holy Communion, baptism, baby or child dedication, holiness, or another topic.

2. For those students who are part of the worship ministry: Make the worship plan for the songs based on the themes of the preaching or the emphasis for the month.

3. Design a survey to evaluate the worship services of the church with the purpose of knowing the congregation's opinion so as to improve the services.

4. Prepare a special worship service using the typical instruments and rhythms of your country with the purpose of appreciating the culture.

5. Prepare a drama with the youth of the church to teach the children the importance of participating in the worship services of the church.

6. Organize a month where each week focuses on a spiritual discipline with the purpose of involving the entire congregation in certain disciplines such as prayer, fasting, visiting the sick, sharing with those in need, etc.

7. With the students that attend the NYI (youth group) and/or the NYI Council, plan services with special themes for either one trimester, one semester or for one year.

8. Design and make a mural that through artistic creativity communicates the lifestyle of a true worshiper.

9. Make bookmarks using Biblical texts that teach worship principles as a lifestyle and hand them out to the congregation or another group.

Lesson 1

WHAT IS WORSHIP?

Objectives

- Define words related to the topic of worship.
- Understand the concept of worship in the Old and New Testaments.
- Understand what it means to live a lifestyle of worship.

Main Ideas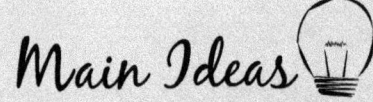

- Worship means to express reverence with the greatest honor and respect to a superior and divine being. It can also be defined as the greatest form of love.
- True worship is that which is wholly concentrated on the Lord.

What do people understand about worship?

Thanksgiving: An attitude of thankfulness to God for what we receive from Him.

Praise: The act of declaring the greatness of God through our words, songs and lives.

Definitions

It is important to know the correct significance of the terminology associated with worship such as the words "praise," "thanksgiving," and "worship" since these terms are often used incorrectly in common usage.

Praise - The word praise means to honor, exalt, glorify, magnify, commend or applaud someone for something. To praise means to verbally express glory and honor to a person who deserves it.

Thanksgiving - Thanksgiving is an expression of gratitude; it means to thank someone.

Worship - Worship means to express reverence with the greatest honor and respect to a being who is considered to be superior and divine. It can also be defined as the greatest form of love. The Hebrew and Greek terminology that is translated in our Bibles as "worship" and/or "to worship" can also be understood as "fear, seek, serve, bow down and minister." Worship, then, is an expression of honor, worship, and service to God as a response to His work of grace in redemption.

A practical and simple distinction between the act of praise and that of worship as expressions of thanksgiving, is that the act of praise emphasises exalting God for his works (what he has done), while worship exalts him for who He is.

Words for Worship in the Old Testament

In the Old Testament, worship is linked to service.

In order to better understand the Biblical basis for worship, it is necessary to study the key terms in the Hebrew language as they are used in the Old Testament. The key terms that define worship are *shachah* and *abad*.

Shachah

Shachah is a Hebrew word in the Old Testament that refers to worship.

School of Leadership - Worship as a Lifestyle

Shachah appears 191 times and in the original sense means: "to worship, bow down, prostrate oneself." Abraham used the word *shachah* when he said in Genesis 22:5, "Stay here with the donkey while I and the boy go over there. We will worship and then we will come back to you" (NIV). The worship of God was associated with the practice of offering sacrifices.

Also, in Genesis chapter 24, Abraham used the word shachah as a description of worship and gratitude to God, "... and I bowed down and worshiped the LORD. I praised the LORD, the God of my master Abraham" (v. 48, NIV); "When Abraham's servant heard what they said, he bowed down to the ground before the LORD" (v. 52, NIV). In this passage, shachah means to bow down to the ground to show worship and reverence or respect toward another human or to God.

For example, in Genesis 33:3, 6-7, *shachah* indicates the humbling and submitting of Jacob and all his family in his reconciliation with his brother Esau: "He himself went on ahead and bowed down to the ground seven times as he approached his brother…Then the maidservants and their children approached and bowed down. Next, Leah and her children came and bowed down. Last of all came Joseph and Rachel, and they too bowed down" (NIV).

This word *shachah* expresses a concept of worship based on reverence. It means to pay homage and to submit to the object of worship. The humbling and bowing down to the ground shows a surrender of the will. It means to give reverence and honor to the one who receives the worship, which implies service and surrender.

The attitude and action of humbling oneself before someone is not common in our modern world. To serve and humble oneself is not a popular attitude. However, given the evidence of the meaning of the Hebrew word *shachah*, this is the first Biblical concept of worship that we should learn. This reality brings us to ask this question: How can humans be worthy to worship God? The answer is that only by His grace can we learn the proper attitude for worship.

Abad

The other Hebrew word for worship is *abad*, which means "worship" as much as "serve." This word occurs almost 300 times in the Old Testament and it describes the action of "working, cultivating, and serving." It is mainly used in the sense of "to work for someone."

There are two passages where we can see examples of the usage of abad. In Genesis 25:23 when Rebecca sought the reason why her twins were fighting in her womb, God responded: "Two nations are in your womb, and two peoples from within you will be separated; one people will be stronger than the other, and the older will serve the younger" (NIV). That is to say that Esau and his descendants would serve and work for Jacob and his descendants.

Shachah: a Hebrew word that means to physically or symbolically bow down before the presence of the majesty and holiness of God. It also indicates the idea of an act of the mind and the body that shows obedience and submission before the will of God.

Ritual: a ceremony or liturgy that forms part of the worship service.

Hundreds of years later, when the people of Israel were in slavery in Egypt, God sent Moses and Aaron to give a message to Pharaoh: "The LORD, the God of the Hebrews, has sent me to say to you: Let my people go, so that they may worship me in the desert" (Exodus 7:16, NIV). It is evident that the word abad expresses the nuance of serving in worship (Deuteronomy 6:13; 11:13, 14).

Words for Worship in the New Testament

In the New Testament, worship describes total surrender to the Lordship of Christ.

Bob Sorge states in his book Exploration of Worship that there are six reasons to worship God:

-Because God's Word commands us to do so.
-Because God is enthroned in worship.
-Because it is good to worship the Lord.
-Because God is worthy of our worship.
-Because God created man and woman to worship Him.
-Because there is power in worship.

In the New Testament we find the Greek term *proskuneo*, which means, "to worship." It is used 60 times in the New Testament and is the word that Jesus used when he taught the Samaritan woman about true worship in John 4:20-24. It is translated in the NIV as *worship* 51 times; as *fall at feet (or knees)* 4 times; as *kneel before (or down)* 4 times; and as *pay homage* once.

The concept of worship contained in the Hebrew word *shachah* in the Old Testament is expressed with the Greek word *proskuneo* in the New Testament. It is formed from two words: *pros*, which means "in front of or before," and *kuneo*, which means, "to kiss." The sense of the Greek word *proskuneo* is clearly the same as that of the Hebrew word *shachah*. It describes the worshiper who humbles him or herself before God. It is interesting to observe that many times in the New Testament the word *proskuneo* appears with the word for "bow down to the ground" (there are examples in Matthew 2:11 and Revelation 7:11).

Consistent with the meaning of these words, we can affirm that Biblical worship is a worship of humility, submission, service, and generosity. It is to prostrate oneself or bow down to the feet of someone, to give a visible demonstration of the superiority of the other and to submit voluntarily to that other person. The worshiper should have an attitude of profound respect and complete humility before the Lord, focusing one's attention only on Him, not on oneself.

Congregational worship should be absolutely and solely the worship of the Lord with an emphasis on Him and only Him. "For from him and through him and to him are all things" (Romans 11:36, NIV).

In the worship service one should eliminate anything that distracts the congregation from their concentration on the Lord and their worship of Him. This could be music that is out of tune, something in the movement or clothing of the musicians, feedback from the sound system, the volume of the speakers or speaker, someone on the platform who is not participating in the worship, room temperature that is too hot or too cold, a lack of hymnals or chorus books, overhead slides with poor spelling or not adequately visible or not keeping up with the singing, a singer's voice that is conspicuous, people talking, people coming in and out of the room, the lighting, etc.

What Elements Are Included in Worship?

Worship includes many elements.

> **Worship:**
> the constant attitude of devotion and praise to God for being who He is and for His works.

One definition of worship says, "Worship is communion with God in which believers, by grace, center their mind's attention and their heart's affection on the Lord, humbly glorifying God in response to His greatness and His Word" (Dr. Bruce Leafblad). This definition touches almost every relevant aspect of worship.

Worship is mutual communication established by the grace of God (Hebrews 10:19-22). The believer has free access to the Heavenly Father because of the work done by Jesus Christ on the cross. Worship begins with an attitude of humility before God; it continues with a confession of our total dependence, seeking His forgiveness; it then continues with a proclamation of his Lordship and greatness, asking His help to know and do His will in our lives, according to the guidance of His Holy Spirit. Worship ends with the commitment and dedication of the believer to obey and honor God with his or her whole being. The best model of worship is in the Lord's Prayer (Matthew 6:9-13).

Worship is not only the musical segment of a worship service but is also present in every moment of daily life. Authentic worship is not a religious act and is not limited to rituals or ceremonies. It does not occur only inside a church building; it does not depend on a place, but worship should permeate everything a Christian thinks, says, does, and feels. Worship includes an attitude of gratitude to God for his blessings of the gifts of life and health.

Worship includes words that express joy as we remember what the Lord has done for us in times past. Worship includes moments of private reflection in which a man or woman appreciates the revelation of God by means of his creation. Worship includes the recognition of the sufficiency of God and our dependence on him in times of prayer. Everything that has been mentioned is not an activity that takes place only in a worship service on a Sunday. Worship is so much more. It is a lifestyle.

Corporate worship of the people of God is also of utmost importance. One of the greatest events in human life is to experience the presence of God manifested in the worship services of the church. It is an experience that is difficult to describe in words; it is a divine-human encounter that transcends every other experience in daily life. King David understood this, and so expressed his desire to be in the house of God: "I rejoiced with those who said to me, 'Let us go to the house of the LORD' " (Psalm 122:1).

On many occasions, David declared his need to be in the presence of the Lord, participating in times of worship with his brothers and receiving instruction and comfort from God. The words of David express his overwhelming desire for God and his desire to give to God true worship, recognizing that even his desire to worship comes from God Himself.

Ten Ways to Worship

In this section we will learn ten ways to express worship to God.

Worship is communion with God in which by grace and humility, the believers center their attention and hearts on the Lord, glorifying God in response to His greatness and His Word.

Despite the indisputable truth that all believers should be worshipers, there tends to be confusion in the churches with respect to what it means to be a worshiper. Many wrongly think that worshiping is singing and is synonymous with music and vice versa. As we will see, music is only one way to worship God.

1. Worship through prayer

The best-known prayer in the Bible is the Lord's Prayer, and it is the model that Jesus taught us in order to direct us to the Father. This prayer expresses worship and helps us to concentrate more on the Lord, rather than making prayer just a list of requests (Matthew 6:9-14; Colossians 4:2).

2. Worship through Bible reading

There are countless Biblical passages where worship is expressed using words. For example, Psalms 117, 121, Revelation 4 and 5, among others, may be verses we use in worship.

3. Worship through obedience

When someone obeys the commandments of the Lord, he or she is giving honor and reverence to Him. The obedience in our lives is more pleasing to God than any ritual: "Does the LORD delight in burnt offerings and sacrifices as much as in obeying the voice of the LORD? To obey is better than sacrifice, and to heed is better than the fat of rams" (1 Samuel 15:22).

4. Worship through tithes and offerings

The tithes and offerings of believers indicate the recognition of his Lordship and show an attitude of willingness and commitment to the Lord. Clearly, this is a form of worship (Genesis 28:22; Matthew 21:1-4).

5. Worship through fellowship

The love between Christian brothers and sisters is a sign to the world that there are people who worship God. Jesus said, "By this all men will know that you are my disciples, if you love one another" (John 13:35, Psalm 133).

6. Worship through evangelism

One of the tasks that the Lord entrusted to us is to evangelize the lost. This was Jesus' mission as well as the disciples' mission. "The Lord is not slow in keeping his promise, as some understand slowness. He is patient with you, not wanting anyone to perish, but everyone to come to repentance" (2 Peter 3:9, see 2 Corinthians 5:18-20).

7. Worship through compassionate ministry

Believers honor their Lord when they compassionately serve those who are in need (Matthew 25:34).

8. Worship through the attitude of gratitude

Gratitude to the Lord is also a form of worship because it is the recognition of his greatness and love. It can be expressed publically as thanksgiving, but what is really important is the attitude (Psalm 103:1-5; 34:1-3).

9. Worship through submission to the Lord

The key to being a genuine worshiper is total surrender to the Lord. This submission allows God to work freely within us, purifying our hearts: "May God himself, the God of peace, sanctify you through and through. May your whole spirit, soul and body be kept blameless at the coming of our Lord Jesus Christ" (1 Thessalonians 5:23).

10. Worship through consecration

God wants his children to be involved in the expansion of his Kingdom, making a difference for others by means of a life of integrity and service. Many people make the mistake of wanting to serve in a ministry of the church without first learning how to worship. For example, whoever leads worship in a church service has to be a good musician, but even though this is important, he or she first has to be someone who genuinely worships God (Deuteronomy 10:8, John 4:21-24).

As we see, true worship is found in the inmost part of the Christian's heart. It flows naturally when there is an attitude of humble submission before our Creator and Lord, an attitude of gratitude for rescuing us from sin, a profound love because He loved us with an everlasting love and a passionate desire to serve Him with all our lives in obedience to His call.

True worship is the natural result of a life of holiness and service.

We should respond personally to the initiative of God. He reveals Himself just as He is, and He wants us to do the same. He tells us the truth and hopes we will follow His example. Through worship, we communicate with God the truth about our thoughts, feelings and desires.

WHAT DID WE LEARN?

The Biblical terms help us to understand that worship goes beyond an activity in a worship service. Genuine worship is a lifestyle of devotion, obedience and service.

Lesson 1 - What is Worship?

Activities

Time 20'

INSTRUCTIONS:

1. In small groups of 3 or 4 people, write a definition of worship in your own words.
   _____
   _____
   _____
   _____
   _____

2. In the same groups, prepare a short skit to represent your definition to the rest of the class. Before performing the skit, each group will read its definition to the rest of the class or write it on the blackboard.

3. What changes are needed in your life to make you a better worshiper?
   _____
   _____
   _____
   _____
   _____

4. Mention at least 5 methods of worship that you would like to incorporate into your life or practice with more frequency from now on.
   _____
   _____
   _____
   _____
   _____

Lesson 2

WORSHIP IN THE OLD TESTAMENT

Objectives

- To understand the principles of worship in the Old Testament.
- To apply these principles to our personal and congregational practice.

Main Ideas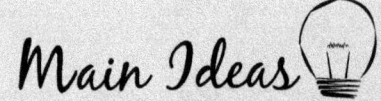

- Worship was a family practice led by the head of the family whose responsibility was to continue the practice from generation to generation.
- God himself taught His people how to worship Him.
- Worship, as a spiritual activity, was God's way of meeting His people.

Worship in the Days of the Patriarchs

In the Old Testament we find valuable principles about worship.

The book of Genesis tells the history of the first generations from the time of the creation of the world (approximately 4000 B.C. until the death of Joseph (1600 AC approximately).

The book of Genesis has many examples of worship offered to God by men like Noah, Abraham, Isaac and Jacob. Noah built an altar to thank God for delivering him from the flood. It was Noah's first act after leaving the ark (Genesis 8:18-20).

Abraham built an altar very close to his tent where he worshiped God. Before, he had built an altar where God had appeared to him (Genesis 12: 7-8). Then he went to the mountains located east of Bethel. He established his camp with Bethel to the west and Ai to the east, and in this place he also built an altar to the Lord and called on His name. Abraham built a new altar every time he moved his dwelling place. Note in Genesis 13:18, that Abraham had a deep longing to have an altar nearby where he could worship God: "So Abram went to live near the great trees of Mamre at Hebron, where he pitched his tents. There he built an altar to the Lord."

In obedience to God, Abraham offered his son Isaac. God stopped the sacrifice and blessed Abraham for his faith and obedience (Genesis 22:9-12). Isaac continued the practice of worship and built an altar to God (Genesis 26:17-18, 23-25).

Altar: A construction made by man where offerings (sacrifices) are made to God. The Hebrew word for altar is related to the word for sacrifice. The first worshipers constructed altars by piling uncut rocks (Exodus 20:24-26). They did it this way to differentiate their altars from the ones of the idol-worshiping nations to their gods.

Jacob, the son of Isaac, continued to worship as his father and grandfather before him. When he purchased new land, he built a new altar and worshiped God there (Genesis 34:18-20). In the greatest trial Jacob faced in his life, God appeared to him and commanded him to build an altar to worship him. This resulted in a great change in Jacob's life, and God greatly blessed him and his offspring (Genesis 36:1-7).

It is evident that these patriarchs taught their family about the ways to worship God. They built altars close to their tents, and took very seriously the task of passing the information onto the next generation, from fathers to sons and to the whole family.

The main principles of worship in the times of the Patriarchs are the following:

Worship in the Time of the Patriarchs			
In the family: • Led by the Father. • Passed on from father to sons to grandsons.	It was intimate and personal: • In response to God's call. • God blesses, protects and guides the worshiper.	It was simple: • It lacked a complex ritual system. • It was God-centered.	Worship was offered in any place: • All was needed was a place to build an altar. • A place close to home.

Patriarch: Male leader of a family or tribe. In the book of Genesis, the leaders who lived between the years 1900 and 1600 B.C. would be considered patriarchs: Abraham, Isaac and Jacob.

Worship in the Mosaic Law

In this section we will consider the worship practices during the time of the Mosaic Law.

Four hundred and fifty (450) years after the Patriarchs, when the sons of Israel where a sufficient number to become a nation, God gave worship instructions through Moses. There is a distinct difference between the worship the Patriarchs practiced and the worship established by Israel as a nation.

When Israel was in the desert (between the exodus from Egypt and the establishment in Canaan), the people met for worship at the tabernacle. In the tabernacle there was the altar for sacrifice and a main tent that was divided into the Holy place and the Most Holy place. The Ark of the Covenant was kept in the Most Holy place. The ark was a box made of wood, finely decorated with gold and it contained the tablets of the covenant law (The Ten Commandments), a jar with a sample of manna (the bread provided by God in the desert), and Aaron's staff (Exodus 16:33-34; Numbers 17:10). There were other objects in the Holy Place including the lampstand, the table on which the bread of the presence was placed, as well as the altar of incense. All of these items had great symbolic meaning reminding the people that the presence of God was with them and that their worship should be constant.

The worship service began when the leader or priest stood before the people with the purpose of leading them into a worship act that was pleasing to God, according to the instructions God himself had given them. It should be highlighted that from then on, worship for the people of Israel became a corporal act with the sacrifice of animals (Exodus 24:1-8).

God's instructions for Moses and the people of Israel were very interesting since they revealed God's plan and intention concerning all the details of the tabernacle of worship.

Tents: Rectangular rooms that were constructed with wood posts and curtains made of leather or weaved animal furs (goats, sheep or camels). According to the size, the structure could be divided inside with other curtains. When it was warm, the sides could be raised to allow for airflow. When it rained or was cold, the structure could be closed so it was airtight. The structure was portable, similar to those used by the Bedouins or that are today used for camping.

Lesson 2 - Worship in the Old Testament

In the times of Moses, worship included three main aspects: specific sacrifices, the tabernacle and an altar that was rich in symbolism.

In Exodus 25:1-2, God gave instructions about choosing an offering. Reflecting about the worship practice in Moses' time, we must remember three important aspects:

- God personally gave to Moses all the instructions about worship, which he shared with the people of Israel.
- Moses made sure that all the instructions given by God were strictly followed.
- God gave rules and practices for worship in a very specific way.

There are many examples of the detailed indications given by God to the priests who ministered the offering of sacrifices for the people.

In Leviticus 6:8-14 we find precise instructions that God gave to the priests.

- The priests were to wear appropriate garments (6:8-11): they had to wear special clothes when they ministered.
- Their whole life was dedicated to keep the fire of the altar burning (6:9, 12 and 13). God commanded that "the fire on the altar must be kept burning" day and night (6:12). The priest was responsible for the fire and for which it represented: the presence of the Lord.
- They were to perform their service reverently, paying close attention to every detail, since God communicates His redemptive plan with His people through each detail.
- They were to be sanctified by God, for His glory, in the presence of the people (Leviticus 10:3-5).
- They were to lead a different lifestyle than all the rest of the people (Leviticus 10:7b-11).

The Tabernacle
- It was constructed in the times of Moses.
- It was a portable sanctuary that was designed like a large camping tent.
- In its interior it held the Ark of the Covenant, and it symbolized the presence of God in the midst of the people.
- The tribes camped around the Tabernacle (Exodus 25 – 31).

In Moses' time, the people of Israel began to celebrate new festivals: there were festivals in gratitude for the harvest, religious festivals like the Day of Atonement, and many others.

For the first time in the Bible, worship is presented as a congregational practice. Furthermore, a ritual system was established that the people had to carefully observe.

Worship in the Times of the Monarchs

King David made a significant contribution as a worshiper with his Psalms.

The time of the kings was another special time in the history of the people of Israel and another period in the evolution of the worship practice. The second King of Israel, David, came to be the most important and influential worshiper in the Old Testament. We can see evidence of this in what he did: he prepared his son to build the temple, and he was a musician and author of great poems and songs to the Lord.

David gave worship an important place in his life and his kingdom. Entire books have been written about the contribution of King David to worship. Nevertheless, there is no doubt that his greatest contribution was the Psalms.

In 2 Samuel 6:12-19, we can see King David as the first and greatest worshiper in all of Israel. As opposed to his predecessor Saul, David recognized the value of having the Ark of the Covenant in the country's capital. He understood that this meant having the presence of God in the midst of the people. For his faith, David and his kingdom received many blessings from God.

Another relevant aspect of King David, which was evident in his life, was his joy in worship. When he finished carrying the ark and celebrating, he gave the people bread, dates and raisins. (II Samuel 6:12-19).

The Book of Psalms is a collection of songs and poems from different authors in Israel. Of all of them, the most prominent is David, who is the author of 73 of the psalms of this "hymn book." We can see David's thinking and his concept of worship if we take into consideration two of his psalms. Psalm 103 is personal. David invites himself to worship God and ends up inviting all of creation to join him in this act of worship.

In Psalm 108:1-5, David includes an example of a worship program. He starts with a steadfast heart, which he describes as an inner willingness that brings the person the opportunity to sing and worship the Lord in the morning. Musical instruments could accompany this worship. It is meant to be shared among the peoples and nations, motivated by God's love and faithfulness, culminating with praise to God in the whole Earth.

King Solomon, David's son, received the mission and the instructions to build the temple as an inheritance from his father (1 Chronicles 28:11-19). The project took seven years. 2 Chronicles 5:1-7 tells about the dedication service for the temple, which was attended by all the people.

The Ark of the Covenant was finally placed in the Most Holy Place of the temple, and afterwards the sacrifices began. Then, Solomon himself prayed to dedicate the temple to the Lord.

It is important to note Solomon's attitude of worship and humiliation. He first knelt down before God in front of all the people of Israel, then he acknowledged that the temple he had built was unworthy of the Lord, and then he spoke from his heart asking God to show mercy and forgive his sins and those of his people (2 Chronicles 6:12-42).

Furthermore, God sealed that moment with a mighty demonstration of his power: fire came down from heaven and consumed the burnt offering and sacrifices on the altar. The glory of the Lord filled the temple in such a way that the priests could not enter the temple. After this, Solomon

Lesson 2 - Worship in the Old Testament

The word Psalms comes from the Greek word psalmos. Originally this word signified to touch or run your fingers over the chords, but it later came to mean a song dedicated to God and accompanied by musical instruments. In Hebrew the word for Psalm is Sefer Tehillim.

Dimensions of the Tabernacle:
The main tent had a rectangular shape of 13.5 m. long by 4.8 m. wide by 4.5 m. high. It was constructed with 48 acacia planks covered in gold and supported with bases made of silver (Exodus 26:25-29).

Burnt offering refers to an offering that was burned completely. Some examples of this are found in Exodus 30:20 and Leviticus 5:12; 23:8, 25, 27.

In Leviticus 10:1-12, we can see that God is demanding where worship is concerned. In this passage, God provides precise instructions so that worship to God is carried out carefully and excellently. When the sons of Aaron took the incense that had been set apart for God and used it for other purposes, they were struck down in the act (Leviticus 10:1,2).

continued to offer sacrifices to dedicate the temple to God by offering 22,000 head of cattle and 120,000 sheep and goats (2 Chronicles 7:1-5).

Worship During the Monarchy		
Community Worship: • Concentrated in a specific place (Hebron, later called Jerusalem). • Worship as a national meeting activity.	Worship expressed through songs: • Collection of Psalms. • A liturgical system is introduced. • Professional musicians dedicated to serving in the temple (Asaph, etc.)	The Northern kingdom divides and builds another temple: • The prophets in this period called on the people in both kingdoms to offer genuine worship.

Psalms of the Pilgrimage

Psalms are an expression of community worship.

When Israel was established in the land of Canaan, everyone looked to Jerusalem as the national place of worship.

It was a moral obligation for each man in Israel to present himself each year before the Priest to offer a sacrifice to God. As a consequence, multitudes of people took long trips to come to this special place for worship that was situated in the mountains of Judah.

Many family members joined the pilgrimages to accompany the men. The excitement of walking to the Holy City turned into at time of community worship that lasted throughout their travels to Jerusalem.

As a result, today we have a section of the Book of Psalms called "Psalms of Ascension" that go from Psalm 120 to 134. These Psalms tell about the joy of the people of God, describe the geographical dangers along the way, mention the adversity of the pilgrimage and tell about the experiences of the faithful as they worshiped at the Temple and observed the priests in their holy duties.

Worship During the Exile and Post Exilic Periods

What was worship like for the Israelites during the time of Exile?

Because of the great amount of sin (idolatry) and the constant rejection of God, the Israelites were deported as slaves to Babylon. During this time, the Israelites did not have a temple, a system for performing sacrifices. They were without the glory and the presence of God.

The invaders pillaged and destroyed the temple (2 Chronicles 36:15). It was during this time that the Israelites began to feel the weight of their sin as they lived so far from home. Through the ministry of the prophets, such as Ezekiel and Jeremiah, God opened the hearts of the people and never again did the people return to worship idols.

In the Psalms, there are many example of worship during this time of exile. One of these is Psalm 137 where one can sense the heartache and the strong desire for vengeance against the enemy. Other prophets, like Daniel, show an attitude of humbleness and repentance. In Daniel 9, we find an intercessory prayer for Israel; one can clearly see the confession of sin of the people of Israel in verses 5 and 6. Also, Daniel ended his prayer asking God for the return of Israel to her territory.

Ezra, Nehemiah and the people of Israel received permission from King Darius and Artaxerxes to return to Canaan where they reconstructed Jerusalem and the temple. It is interesting to study the worship of the people of Israel during this time in the book of Nehemiah, chapter 8:1-12.

In summary, the characteristics of worship in the exile and post exile are these:

√ Israel understood that they should serve only God – the one true God – and that they should leave behind all idolatry; they understood that God would protect them from the pagan nations if they would stay firm and faithful in their service to God.

√ Following the destruction of the temple, synagogues were established for worship and the study of the Word. Each congregation had a minimum of ten families.

The Bible highlights the influence of David as a Psalmist in II Samuel 23:1,2.

Praise the Lord, my soul;
all my inmost being, praise his holy name.
Praise the Lord, my soul,
and forget not all his benefits—
who forgives all your sins
and heals all your diseases,
who redeems your life from the pit
and crowns you with love and compassion,
who satisfies your desires with good things
so that your youth is renewed like the eagle's.
Psalm 103:1-5 (NIV)

With all my heart
I praise the Lord,
and with all that I am
I praise his holy name!
With all my heart
I praise the Lord!
I will never forget
how kind he has been.
The Lord forgives our sins,
heals us when we are sick,
and protects us from death.
His kindness and love
are a crown on our heads.
Each day that we live,
he provides for our needs
and gives us the strength
of a young eagle.
Psalm 103:1-5
(Contemporary English Version)

What Did We Learn?

We learned about the principles of worship in the Old Testament and the characteristics of worship in the different time periods in the life of the people of Israel.

Lesson 2 - Worship in the Old Testament

Activities

Time 20'

INSTRUCTIONS:

1. We have studied that Abraham built altars for worship close to his dwelling place. What practical teaching can we derive from this practice for our lives today?
   _____
   _____
   _____

2. What were the responsibilities of the head of the family in terms of passing on the faith to future generations? Do you think that this is an important responsibility today? Explain why.
   _____
   _____
   _____

3. It is a fact that God gave precise instructions on how to worship in Moses' time. What does this teach us about how we should worship in a way that is pleasing to God?
   _____
   _____
   _____

4. Choose 5 verses of Psalm 103 to translate into your own words and make them your own prayer.
   _____
   _____
   _____
   _____
   _____

5. Write a personal reflection about what the Lord teaches us through the prophet Micah in chapter 6:6-8 in terms of our attitude when approaching God as worshipers.
   _____
   _____
   _____
   _____
   _____

Lesson 3

WORSHIP IN THE NEW TESTAMENT

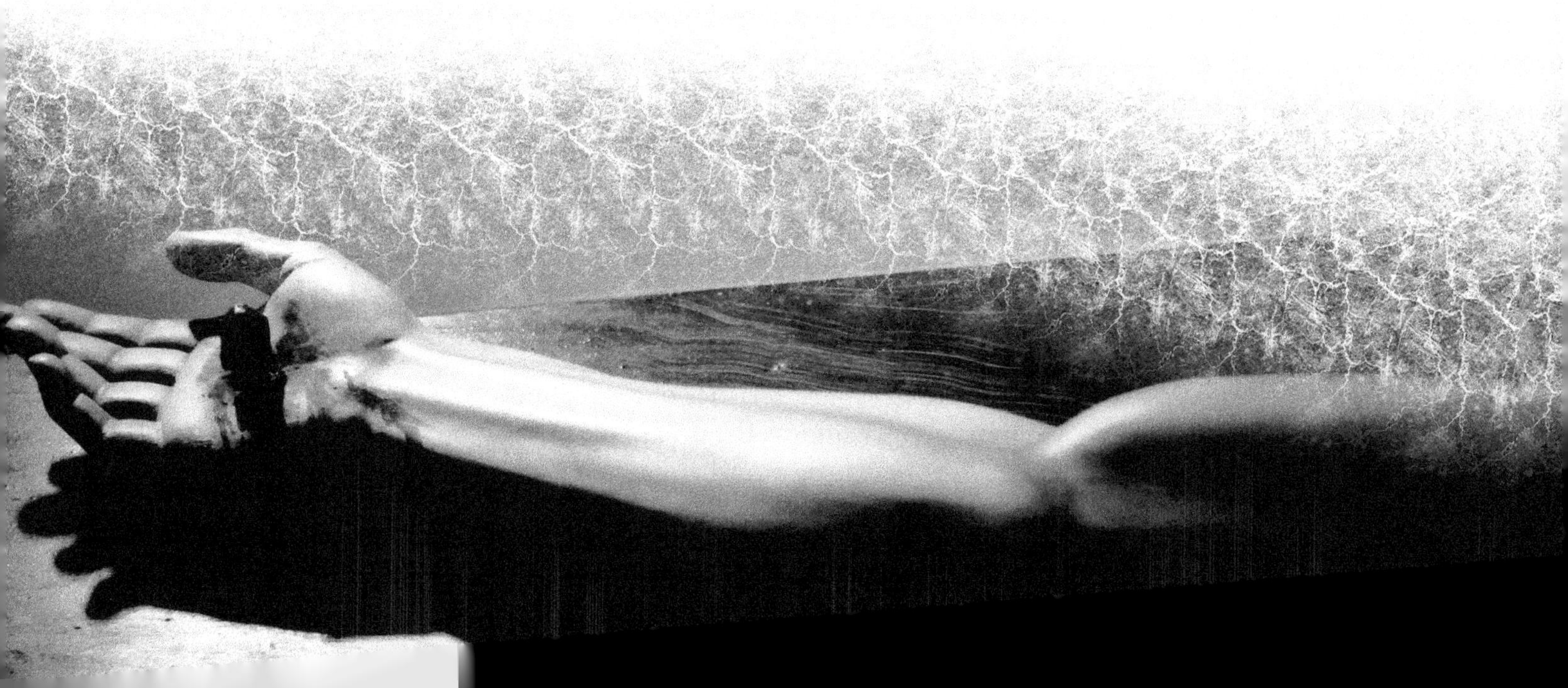

Objectives

- To understand the teaching of Jesus concerning worship.
- To identify the principles of worship in the book of Acts, the Pauline Letters and Revelation.

Main Ideas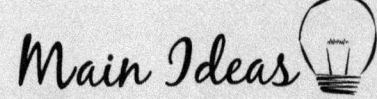

- Worship of the Lord should be sincere and always guided by the Holy Spirit who lives in our hearts.
- The New Testament emphasizes the importance of meeting together in worship with other believers.

John Wesley in his Notes on the New Testament translates the sentiment of the words of Jesus in John 4:22 in this way: "Ye Samaritans are ignorant, not only of the place, but of the very object of worship."

How do you know if your acts of worship or service to God are genuine?

Introduction

There is a tendency to think that the New Testament does not say much about worship; however, that is not true. The New Testament does speak about worship, especially in the teachings of Jesus and the Apostle Paul. In Acts, we also find very valuable information concerning the worship in the early church. Finally in the book of Revelation we find excellent examples of worship.

The Temple and the Synagogue

The Temple and the synagogues were important to the Jews.

During the ministries of John the Baptist and Jesus, the Temple, reconstructed by Herod, was in use. The sacrificial system and the ministry of the priests held an important position of status in the Jewish culture of that time.

However, beginning with the Babylonian exile, things changed greatly. Worship and Jewish education was no longer centered in the Temple, but rather in the synagogues. The synagogue's purpose was to provide spiritual education to the Jewish families during the exile and to offer a location for to worship God. Consequently, it was the synagogue that became the central point of influence in the religious life of the Jewish community.

One of the characteristics of the institution of the synagogue and its impact on Judaism was the difference in the type of worship and liturgy, which was in contrast to what had been offered to God in the Temple.

In summary, worship in the synagogue was more direct and simple. In the synagogue, there was an opportunity for dialogue, participation, and the possibility of spontaneous demonstrations of joy and praise. Every Jew had the opportunity to repeat Psalms and pray.

Jesus and Worship

What are the principles taught by Jesus about worship?

In the Gospel of John, we read the story of Jesus when he explained to the Samaritan women the meaning of true worship (John 4:19-24). First of all, Jesus makes it clear that to God the place in which the worshiper is located is not of great importance. This issue was disputed between Jews and Samaritans for generations.

Both the Jews and the Samaritans wanted their nation to be the center for worship. The Samaritans wanted the center for worship to be in the Mount Gerizim, and the Jews wanted it in the Temple in Jerusalem. Jesus knew very well that worship did not depend on location since God's Spirit is in all places. This is very important considering that the first Christians lived in a time when the Temple had been destroyed and there was no central place where they could go to worship God.

John 4:19-24 reveals that true worship is based on knowing the truth. Knowing God and his essence is central to being able to worship God in a way that pleases Him. In John 4:23, Jesus also taught the Samaritan woman how real worshipers worshipped, and He pointed out two important aspects.

The first is that real worshipers worship in "the Spirit and in truth." This means that we come before Him in total honesty, hiding nothing, and without pretense (Psalms 51:6).

The second aspect of this teaching is that it is God Himself who wants this kind of worshipper. God does not accept sacrifices and offerings if the worshipper does not come to Him in a right spirit (John 4:23).

Finally, Jesus said that "God is spirit, and his worshipers must worship in the Spirit and in truth" (John 4:24). The phrase "his worshipers" makes us think that there are those who do not worship Him.

God has given us free will; God does not force anybody to worship Him. But there will come a day when every knee will bow before Him (Isaiah 45:23, Philippians 2:10). The Holy Spirit, who dwells within our hearts, must guide all true worship to the Lord.

The Teachings of Jesus about Public and Private Worship

In Matthew 6:1, Jesus teaches about how public and private worship of God should be related. The test of the genuineness of our worship is found in how we worship when we are alone, which is to say, the worship that flows naturally throughout daily life. Jesus referred, for example, to offerings for the poor, prayer and fasting, which are all forms of worship in public, just as they are forms of worship in private (Matthew 6:2-3 and 16-17). Jesus

What is the importance of the sacraments of Baptism and the Lord's Supper in our spiritual growth?

Many Biblical experts indicate that the breaking of the bread was an explicit illustration of the abusive treatment of the body of Jesus before his death. If the broken bread represented his body, his disciples could not have misunderstood the reality of his soon approaching death.

Lesson 3 - Worship in the New Testament

always encouraged His listeners to maintain a strong devotional life, both publically and privately.

The Establishment of Baptism by Jesus (Matthew 3:15)

The Sacraments of Baptism and the Lord's Supper are important to our Christian growth and worship.

Jesus instituted baptism in water when he presented himself before John the Baptist to be baptized in the Jordan River. The conversation between John and Jesus teaches us that baptism is an act of obedience and a privilege for each believer. "…It is proper for us to do this to fulfill all righteousness" (Matt 3:15).

Every new believer should be baptized in a public act to give testimony of his or her confession of sin and new life in Christ. Baptism is an important step forward in the spiritual life and should not be taken lightly. Baptism is an outward symbol of the work that the Holy Spirit has done in our hearts to take away our sins and give us new life as sons and daughters of God. Baptism of new believers became a common practice in the history of the church because of the commandment given by Jesus (Matthew 28:16-20).

The Establishment of the Lord's Supper (Matthew 26:26-30; Mark 14:22-25 and Luke 22:19-20)

These passages narrate the establishment of the Lord's Supper. Each scripture relates the testimony of a different person as they experience the same thing. Each act of Jesus in this supper is significant because (1) Jesus celebrated the Feast of the Passover with his disciples, being that it is the most significant of all the Jewish feasts. (2) Jesus used the bread and the cup from the supper as "visual aids" to talk about the significance of his death (see Isaiah 53:3-5).

Worship in the Book of Acts

How did the Early Church worship?

At the beginning of the Book of Acts we see that the Christians in the Early Church continued to be involved in the religious practices of Judaism because they had the hope that the Jews would embrace the teachings of Jesus.

They hoped that the Jews would understand that Jesus Christ was the Messiah that God had promised since the time of Abraham, and that they would become part of this new movement. For this reason in the beginning of the church, the disciples of Jesus continued going to the Temple of Jerusalem and fulfilled the Jewish religion customs.

Jesus answered, "For now this is how it should be, because we must do all that God wants us to do. So Jesus was baptized. And as soon as he came out of the water, the sky opened, and he saw the Spirit of God coming down on him like a dove" (Matthew 3:15,16 in the Contemporary English Version).

Why did Jesus have to be baptized? According to G. Campbell Morgan, the baptism of Jesus was a public act in which the Savior identified with all sinners. His baptism was an act by which he consented to taking the place of sinners.

The first Christians felt a duty to preach the gospel to those of their own race who worshiped the same God. So, the apostles taught the gospel to the Jews in the synagogues. They did not build another temple, nor did they construct separate synagogues. In the beginning it went well for them as they were welcomed into the synagogue and given the opportunity to speak. (Acts 13:14-15).

According to first century historians, there were places where Jews lived where there were no synagogues. Some Jews had the custom of meeting to pray and worship the name of Christ at the edge of the river (Acts 16:13). The importance of meeting together with other believers to worship was established from the very beginning of the Church.

How did the first Christians worship God? The first Christians went to the Temple of Jerusalem (John 10:23; Acts 2:46; 3:1, 8, 11; 4:1-6; 5:12).

Worship in the Pauline Letters

The Teachings of Paul Concerning Worship

In his letters, Paul taught the churches about worship. Some are of the opinion that 1 Corinthians chapters 11 and 14 are answers from the apostle to questions about the practice of worship in the services or gatherings of the congregations. For example, this letter describes various special situations: if women should cover their head during the worship time (11:2-16); the abuses in the Last Supper (11:17-34); and the theme of spiritual gifts and how to use them (chapters 12 and 14).

Paul approaches these problems from a pastoral point of view, beginning with Biblical principles and a clear understanding of what is significant in a personal relationship with Christ. At the time, there where common cultural practices such as the use of a veil for women, the practice of speaking in other languages in the services, among other issues, which caused disorder and frustration in the meetings. Paul confronted these practices that were destroying the unity and fellowship of the people and weakening the character of Christ that should be reflected in the lives of Christians.

***Proskuneo** in Greek is usually translated as worship. But occasionally it is translated with the verb "postrate onself" such as in Matthew 8:2; 9:18; 15:25 and others.*

Another important aspect regarding worship in the Pauline Epistles is the profound significance of the Greek word *koinonia*, which signifies a profound social union much deeper than the word friendship indicates. J. Donald Butler defines *koinonia* as a "friendship involving the Spirit" which enlightens and deepens each relationship of the believer, and even more so the friendship between brothers and sisters in Christ (1 Corinthians 10:16, Philippians 1:5).

The significance of *koinonia* also touches the life of each believer through personal worship. We see this in the experience of the Apostle Paul in his conversion experience when his faith was transformed in such a way that Christ became everything to him: his life, his Lord, his model, his light, his

***Proskuneo** is found 48 times in the New Testament. Twenty-three of those 48 times are found in Revelation.*

Lesson 3 - Worship in the New Testament

judge and his eternal glory. He said, *"I have been crucified with Christ and I no longer live, but Christ lives in me. The life I live in the body, I live by faith in the Son of God, who loved me and gave himself for me"* (Galatians 2:20).

His life and ministry were characterized by a Christ-centered vision. He understood the church to be the body of Christ and our bodies to be the temple of the Holy Spirit, which led to the logical conclusion that we belong to Christ. He taught that when a believer enters into a personal relationship with Christ (conversion), the result is a new creature created in the image of Christ.

In Galatians 5:25 and Romans 8, we find an explanation of what it means to *"walk in the Spirit"* and *"live in the Spirit."* When Christ lives in the hearts of believers, their way of living responds to this new authority and guidance. The Spirit guides their lives. The Spirit enters into the very existence of the believer (2 Corinthians 3:3).

The Apostle also developed the theme of freedom from sin, using worship as his context. He explains that freedom is not obtained through human effort, but instead through voluntary and complete giving of self to Jesus Christ to serve him. This same freedom is to be used for the benefit of all members of the body of Christ (Galatians 5:1,13). Paul interprets and applies this liberty in relationship to Christ. To be apart from Christ is to be in "the flesh" and a slave to the law of sin, living out of the will of God (1 Corinthians 1:30, 31).

The Apostle recommends to the Church in Ephesus: "Speak to one another with psalms, hymns and spiritual songs. Sing and make music in your heart to the Lord, always giving thanks to God the Father for everything, in the name of our Lord Jesus Christ (Ephesians 5:19-20). "Spiritual songs" (*ose pneumatikos*) in Greek literally means "songs of the breath of God." This means that the Holy Spirit inspired these spontaneous songs.

Worship in the Book of Revelation

The Book of the Revelation has wonderful descriptions of worship.

In Revelation 5:12, the multitude worshiped Christ: "Worthy is the Lamb, who was slain, to receive power and wealth and wisdom and strength and honor and glory and praise."

The Book of Revelation has many descriptions of worship that are worth noting because they are excellent examples of heavenly worship. In Revelation 5:11-14 there is a detailed description of worship around the throne of God. In almost every chapter of this book there are examples of praise and worship.

The worshipers give glory, honor and thanksgiving to God (4:9), singing "The Song of Moses and the Lamb" (chapter 5 and 15:3). In 5:8, "the four living creatures and the twenty-four elders fell down before the Lamb. Each one had a harp and they were holding golden bowls full of incense, which are the prayers of the saints." In 7:11-12, all the angels and the elders and the living beings fall on their faces before God.

The Book of Revelation teaches that a fundamental aspect of worship is that God is the only one worthy of worship in the entire universe. In chapter 4, verse 11 everyone says these words: "You are worthy, our Lord and God, to receive glory and honor and power, for you created all things, and by your will they were created and have their being." God is worthy to receive all worship because He is the Creator and our Savior.

In the New Testament, it is clear that only God the Father, Son and Holy Spirit are worthy to receive worship.

What Did We Learn?

The principles of worship in the New Testament help us to appreciate that worship is both a necessity and a priority in a believer's life that must be based upon a close and personal relationship with Jesus Christ.

Lesson 3 - Worship in the New Testament

Activities

Time 20'

INSTRUCTIONS:

1. Ask yourself this question: Do I consider myself a true worshiper according to the teachings of Jesus in John 4:19-24?

___

2. Make a list of two or three of your favorite Christian songs. Analyze the words of the songs. Could you say that the words worship God? Is the word choice good? Why?

___

3. Write a brief testimony of your personal experience with baptism and Holy Communion, especially concerning how the sacraments have supported your growth in the faith.

___

4. In groups of three or four, prepare a small survey to evaluate the "koinonia" in your local church.

___

5. In the same small groups, respond to this question: How can we teach new believers to be true worshipers?

___

Lesson 4

WORSHIP AS A LIFESTYLE

Objectives
- To understand the significance of worship as a lifestyle.
- To know the characteristics of a true worshiper.
- To apply those principles to life in a practical way, and in doing so, evaluate our commitment to God.

Main Ideas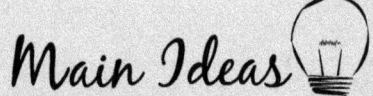
- Worship as a lifestyle has to do with those values, principles and beliefs that bring our lives in focus with God's purposes.
- True worshipers have a mission to serve in the local church, in their community and in the world, reflecting the character and Lordship of Christ in their lives.

What is a lifestyle?
Lifestyle refers to how one understands his or her existence. This understanding results in a way of being, living and relating with others.

Introduction

Upon examining the Biblical principles about worship, one learns that worship is not simply an act or an expression of praise, but something much deeper that is reflected in the way one lives. It has both moral and spiritual implications.

This lesson is an attempt to help the believer respond to the following questions: What values drive my life in each area in which I am developing as an individual? What qualities and habits of my life identify me as a true worshiper? On what Biblical principles am I basing my conduct, faith, obedience, service and praise to God?

Worship and Obedience

A lifestyle of worship is based on knowing God's Word.

Worship as a lifestyle has to do with those values, principles and beliefs that help us to focus our lives on the Person and the purpose of God.

Many people think it is possible to worship God and at the same time live a lifestyle that is indifferent and that lacks commitment to God. Some even go so far as to continue living a sinful life.

The Gospels tell about the moment when Satan tempted Jesus. Satan's intention was to distract Jesus from his mission and from His focus on true worship. *"Jesus said to him, 'Away from me, Satan! For it is written:"Worship the Lord your God, and serve him only"'"* (Matthew 4:10).

False worship results from not knowing God's Word or from being indifferent to the Word. True worship is an internal, spiritual focus in an intimate and personal relationship with God.

Worship as a lifestyle has to do with accepting the Lordship of Christ and submitting to the teaching of the Word. As a result, the worship of the believer is in full agreement with his or her conduct. This is because all true worship is a result of a spiritual change that transforms the life from the inside out (2 Corinthians 5:17).

The God that created us is reflected in our lives in the way we live.

Worship in the Spirit

What does it mean to worship in the Spirit?

John 4:24 says, "God is spirit, and his worshipers must worship in the Spirit and in truth." This passage helps us to understand that there is true worship and false worship. True worship has two fundamental characteristics: worship in Spirit and worship in truth.

Worshiping in spirit signifies that worship is an activity that comes from the spiritual depth of one's being. However, our bodies, minds and emotions also participate in the act of worship.

The Bible teaches that human beings were created in the image and likeness of God, and therefore they have the capacity to enter into communion with the Creator through the spirit, which allows us to respond to God. Mary, the mother of Jesus, expressed that in this verse: "My soul glorifies the Lord and my spirit rejoices in God my Savior" (Luke 1:47).

This verse demonstrates that true worship involves the spiritual, mental and emotional faculties; the act of worship involves all of our being.

Worship "in spirit" requires sincerity of heart, mind, and attitude, as well as genuinely expressing reverence to God. Worship in spirit is more than just an external ritual; it is the spirit of the man or woman in communion with the Spirit of God.

Values: qualities, ideals and norms that guide a person or institution. Life, as a divine gift, has supreme value. Men and women are responsible before their Creator for their conduct and the way they administer their lives.

Worship in Truth

What does it mean to worship in truth?

To worship in truth refers to the quality of the worship. Quality worship is distinguished by the following:

Worship is Based on the Knowledge of God's Nature (Luke 24:17-48; Ephesians 3:14-19)

True worship involves the mind. This means that the worshiper understands who God is in regard to His nature, His work and His character. Jesus came so that the people would know God through his life, his teachings and his work of salvation on the cross.

Lesson 4 - Worship as a Lifestyle

Jesus knew that there would not be true worship if there were not a significant understanding of what is believed and worshiped. One cannot truly worship something or someone that they do not know. For this reason, Jesus took time to teach his disciples that He had come to fulfill the Scriptures. He opened their eyes and their minds so they could understand who He was and the reason that He did all He did.

We were created with the need to intimately know the Creator. The person who lacks this intimacy with God will not be truly happy. Worship is programmed into our human nature, and for this reason human beings always have some object or subject to worship. Sadly, for lack of understanding, many people worship false gods that cannot save them, nor fill their spiritual need.

Worship Should be Focused on Jesus Christ
(Acts 17:24-31; Romans 8:5,6)

> *The God in which we believe is reflected in the lives we live.*

Worship is a result of an intimate relationship with God that is gained through a personal encounter with Christ. Worship is based on communion with Christ through the Word, prayer, meditation, service, private worship and congregational worship.

John 14:6 explains who Jesus is in terms of His nature, His character and His purpose for human beings: Jesus answered, "I am the way and the truth and the life. No one comes to the Father except through me." In the same way, the book of Acts declares: "Salvation is found in no one else, for there is no other name under heaven given to mankind by which we must be saved" (Acts 4:12).

What is the reason why worship must be centered on Jesus Christ? The simple reason is because He is the only true God. He is the Truth, and outside of Him, every act of worship expressed by a human being is considered idolatry.

Worship Should be Based on the Word
(Psalm 119:97-105; 1 John 5:1-13)

> *The worship of God is one of the purposes for which mankind was created (Isaiah 43:6,7 and Ephesians 1:12).*

It is not enough to sincerely worship; one must worship according to the truth of the Word of God. Regarding this, a set of three questions is pertinent: Who do you worship? Why do you worship? How do you worship? The Bible, as the source of authority, revelation and truth, explains to us how humans should come close to God and express worship to the Creator and Redeemer. The Bible gives the correct fundamentals that work in the human's mind and spirit and allow worship that is free of self-centeredness and selfishness.

True worship is not born out of what man considers valuable and sacred, from mankind's life philosophy or from what most satisfies humans' needs, but instead it is born out of what the Bible says about God and human beings. John 17:17b says, "Your word is truth." True worship is strengthened when one learns more about God from the study of His Word.

Worship Has the Purpose of Pleasing God
(1 Corinthians 4:2)

One who worships God is a source of blessing to others.

The motivations of our heart should be sincere, not based on appearances, but instead based only on the intention of pleasing God in all that we do in our daily lives. For example, speaking the truth, being honest at our workplace, being loyal to our Christian convictions and being holy in our interpersonal relationships in marriage, family, church and work are all pleasing to God.

As already mentioned, this has to do with both internal and external integrity of the believer, and the following phrase can be used to explain this: be faithful to God in everything. This means that the concrete actions of our lives should demonstrate our worship of God to the world. (Psalm 24:3-4).

Obedience is the highest form of worship; it clearly demonstrates to God how much we love and respect Him. "…To obey is better than sacrifice, and to heed is better than the fat of rams" (1 Samuel 15:22).

How Can I Become a Better Worshiper?

In this section we will view a practical guide to being better worshipers.

1. Focus your worship on God.

The entire plan of our worship times, whether individual or congregational, should be designed to focus our attention on God and concentrate on Him.

Worshiping in the spirit occurs when a man or woman's spirit communicates with the Spirit of God.

Worship should not be focused on what I will receive, but instead on what I express to God with all of my being, based on who God is. "Praise the Lord, my soul; all my inmost being, praise his holy name" (Psalm 103:1).

The life of the true worshiper is centered in who God is and His purposes. It is pertinent for each church to take the time to evaluate the distinct elements of the service (preaching, congregational prayer, focus of the songs, celebration of Holy Communion, music, offering) and ask this question: Does the way in which the church implements these moments in the service really bring glory to God?

Remember that worship is the natural response of the believer's heart when there is a clear understanding of the presence and character of God.

Are your goals and aspirations centered in God's nature and purposes?

Lesson 4 - Worship as a Lifestyle

Biblical Examples of Lifestyles of Worship:
Job - Job 1:20
David – 2 Samuel 12:20

God delights in the lifestyle of worshippers; nothing pleases Him more than the quality of life displayed by a worshipper. It is our duty; then, to endeavor to please Him by learning to become increasingly Christ like in every way (Sorge, 1987).

"To worship is to quicken the conscience by the holiness of God, to feed the mind with the truth of God, to purge the imagination by the beauty of God, to open the heart to the love of God, to devote the will to the purpose of God" (William Temple, Readings in St. John's Gospel).

2. Commit yourself to live a holy life.

In the Scriptures, there is profound evidence that the person who comes close to God should be separated from all evil. The nature of God demands this. (1 Peter 1:16). Everyone who wants to come close to God should have the desire or need for holy living.

Holiness is the opposite of the sinful life. It can be understood as loving God with all our being, obeying him in everything and serving Him with all our strength. Worship of God should come from a pure heart that is full of the holy love of God. The author of Hebrews declares that holiness is a condition for seeing God (Hebrews 12:14). Holiness is not only a doctrine; it is the basis of a victorious life, rich with the presence of God. It is living according to Christ's example.

Worship that is pleasing to God comes from a holy life. The Apostle Paul says that mankind should lift up "holy hands without anger or disputing" (1 Timothy 2:8).

Our relationships with others should be motivated by love (Matthew 5:24, 1 John 4:20). In the same way, the Bible teaches that a husband should treat his wife with respect, honoring her, so that nothing will hinder his prayers. (1 Peter 3:7).

3. Worship both privately and in community

Some people believe that true worship is demonstrated only in a congregational setting, but they do not understand that the secret of public worship is in the private devotion of the believers, which is characterized first and foremost by an intense prayer life (Matthew 6:6).

The Bible teaches that private worship is very important to spiritual growth (Exodus 29:38-39; Psalm 55:17; Daniel 6:10).

Many Christians these days believe that they can be true worshipers without congregating with a local church. We should not minimize the healthy effects of collective worship. The regular meetings, the order of the service, and the discipline to attend each service are expressions of our personal faith in God. Collective worship is so much richer when it comes out the experience of a daily, intentional encounter with God.

4. Serve others.

The Biblical words for worship and service come from the same root. Both are used in relation to serving God, whether it is in the church or in daily life. This allows us to understand that when God calls us and seeks us to have an intimate relationship with Him, this is not in place of Him assigning us a divine task to serve others (see Matthew 28:17-20). We are called to be nothing less than the incarnation of His love.

We should not confuse activity with worship or service if it is not based on a personal relationship with Christ.

The Apostle Paul warns about the uselessness of giving away all your material goods, giving food to the poor or even giving your body as a sacrifice, if there is not love. (1 Corinthians 13:3).

There are people that neglect love in their desire to serve the Lord. Jesus referred to this when He said, "For it is written: 'Worship the Lord your God, and serve him only" (Matthew 4:10). Therefore, dedicating all your time to serving others never substitutes for worship.

> "This is the secret to a lifestyle of worship – doing everything as if you were doing it for Jesus and by carrying on a continual conversation with him while you do it" (Warren, The Purpose Driven Life).

> "Worship is the believer's response of all that they are - mind, emotions, will, body - to what God is and says and does." (Wiersbe).

What Did We Learn?

A lifestyle of worship consists in a life focused on God and His purposes. It is a life that nurtures a living and personal relationship with Jesus Christ, that is full of God's love and that keeps far from sin. True worshipers have a mission to serve the church, their communities and their nation, reflecting the character of Christ and His Lordship in their lives.

Lesson 4 - Worship as a Lifestyle

Activities

Time 20'

INSTRUCTIONS:

1. Ask yourself this question: Have you ever felt a strong sense of the presence of God when you were worshiping Him privately or publically? When did this occur?
   _____
   _____
   _____

2. Evaluate: How focused are you at this moment on the values, principles and purposes of God?
   _____
   _____
   _____
   _____

3. Write a personal reflection about the following definition: "Worship is your spirit responding to God's Spirit...God-pleasing worship is deeply emotional and deeply doctrinal" (Rick Warren, page 101, 102).
   _____
   _____
   _____
   _____

4. Class Activity: Negotiating Definitions
For each of the following steps, allow one minute of time.

First Step: Each student write a short definition (in their own words and in no more than 12 words) in response to this question: What is the lifestyle of worship?

Second Step: In groups of two, review the two definitions and negotiate to write only one.

Third Step: In groups of four (join two groups from above), negotiate once again to write one definition.

Fourth Step: Repeat the process with 8 students in a group.

Fifth Step: Each group name a representative who will negotiate with the representative of the other groups in order to write just one definition for the entire class. (No more than 12 words). Write it on the board for all to read.

Lesson 5

Congregational Worship

Objectives

- To study the worship elements in a service.
- To know the importance of planning a service.
- To decide upon the standards for the planning of a worship service.

Main Ideas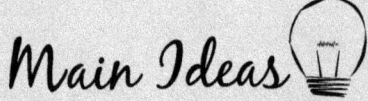

- A good worship plan allows the Holy Spirit to work, transforming the congregation.
- A wise worship plan organizes the service elements in a meaningful way to bless the lives of the worshipers.

There are many aspects to consider in the planning of a worship service. It is necessary to think about the general purpose of each service and plan for each moment. In addition, it is important to consider the needs of the church and the circumstances facing the congregation.

Introduction

Among the many ways to express worship, it is worth our time to highlight the concept of congregational worship, where the church unites and celebrates the greatness of God.

An excellent worship service does not happen on its own but is a product of the effort and concern of the Pastor, the leaders and the congregation.

The Purpose of the Church Service

It is necessary to define the purpose of each worship service.

Each service should have a purpose or objective. It is important to ask these questions: What are the purposes of the services we have in our church? Will we have evangelistic services, sanctification services, holiness services, celebration services, Holy Communion or Baptism services, among others?

It is important that the communion and baptism celebrations be very special services, instead of just including these events as part of a regular program of service. These sacraments require that we give the necessary special attention due to them. These sacraments should be placed appropriately in the service because of their great significance and purpose for spiritual growth.

The service should be integrated. That is to say, each moment should be somehow related to the theme. In a funeral service, for example, the service should be arranged in such a way that the believers receive a message of consolation and hope.

The service should have a logical progression in the elements of the service, organized in such a way that the congregation can concentrate on the central objective. Lacking coherence takes away from the significance of the service. A song can be useful to prepare the heart and mind of

The meeting together of the believers in the name of the Lord Jesus Christ is a sacred event that is worthy of celebrating with excellence since it is Jesus Christ himself who summons us together.

the believer to listen to and discern the message of the preacher. A complementary Bible reading can help the congregation to understand the point of a sermon. A series of songs or a specific testimony can have a profound and edifying effect on the church.

It is beneficial when the leaders and the worship team periodically evaluate the development and use of each element of the service in order to identify the strengths and weaknesses so as to improve.

Program Order in the Congregational Worship Service

Each moment of the worship service should be planned with specific objectives in mind.

To design an order of service that exalts Christ and contributes to church growth, the following list of objectives should be considered.

Specific Objectives that the church service should include:

- Provide moments to encounter God through praise and worship.
- Provide a time of meditation and confession of sin.
- Have a time to celebrate and give thanks.
- Minister through prayer for the needs of the church.
- Provide opportunities to give (offerings) and receive (affirmation).
- Give opportunities to respond through commitment and consecration.

Each one of these specific objectives deserves an explanation; however, for lack of space, we will mention just a few in particular.

Time of Meditation and Confession

Believers and non-believers need the time and opportunity to reflect about their lives and to pray for their spiritual needs. It does not have to be carried out in the same way each week. The time given should be in direct proportion to the needs of the congregation. The purpose of this time is that believers can evaluate their lives and ask forgiveness if they have offended God in their thoughts, words or actions during the week.

Moments of Celebration

In a service there should be opportunities to celebrate the joy of being followers of Christ and being part of His community. Each Sunday, the church celebrates the resurrection of Jesus, which occurred the first day of the week. Through the trials, tests and difficulties of life, the church has many reasons to celebrate.

"We believe in the Church, the community that confesses Jesus Christ as Lord, the covenant people of God made new in Christ, the Body of Christ called together by the Holy Spirit through the Word. God calls the Church to express its life in the unity and fellowship of the Spirit; in worship through the preaching of the Word, observance of the sacraments, and ministry in His name; by obedience to Christ, holy living, and mutual accountability (Manual, Church of the Nazarene, Articles of Faith, #11).

Thanksgiving: A response of the people of God to the grace (undeserved gift) that is received from God.

Liturgy: a set of words, music, and actions regularly used in religious ceremonies.

The believers cannot worship with freedom when they are not in right relationship with the Lord. The times of worship and prayer in the service are good times to receive His forgiveness, even before the message or preaching begins.

Opportunities for Thanksgiving

When God works in the lives of believers it is natural to give thanks and praise as a response to the grace received. The service should provide moments to express this gratitude. The church leaders should guide the congregation in showing the variety of ways to express thanks to God.

Opportunities to Give and Receive

Believers have the deep need to be consoled and encouraged in their faith. They need the strength of their beliefs because each day they encounter many temptations and negative spiritual and worldly forces that make them doubt and consider abandoning the faith. After receiving strength to resist "the lust of the flesh, the lust of the eyes, and the pride of life," they need to hear words of life and comfort for their souls through the Word of God and the words of His servants (1 John 2:16).

The Bible Reading

The Bible reading should occupy a very important place in the service. It should be done with respect and excellence. The reader should read well and have a good voice and pronunciation. The different types of Bible readings such as poems, stories, dramas, etc. should be read appropriately. The correct reading of a passage should lead the reader and the listeners to reflect on God's Word, so it is advisable to read a version that is understandable to the congregation.

The Importance of the Altar in the Worship Service

Every sermon should encourage the listeners to make a commitment to God through prayer at the altar. For example, in a sermon about the call to ministry, many will hear the voice of God inviting them to consecrate their lives to God. This moment is important for their lives, and therefore should be given a special part of the program and planned with much care.

Here is a model of a church service on a Sunday morning:

	Time	Content	Observations
1.	10:00 to 10:05	Musical Prelude	
2.	10:05 to 10:10	Invocation	Prayer of dedication for the service
3.	10:10 to 10:15	Congregational Singing	To concentrate the mind on God
4.	10:15 to 10:20	Pastoral Prayer	
5.	10:20 to 10:50	Praise and Worship	
6.	10:50 to 10:55	Bible Reading	
7.	10:55 to 11:00	Tithes and Offerings	
8.	11:00 to 11:15	Special Activity	This might be a children's presentation or Communion, etc.
9.	11:15 to 11:50	Preaching	
10.	11:50 to 12:05	Altar Call	
11.	12:05 to 12:10	Benediction	
12.	12:10 to 12:15	Musical Postlude	

The worship service or preaching should never be used to discipline believers. When someone needs correction, it is much more effective and correct to confront the person in a personal and private way.

The Importance of Planning

An excellent worship service results from good planning.

The responsibility of those who plan the church service is to create an environment conducive to worshiping in spirit and in truth. The Pastor and the worship team should work together to plan a good worship service, recognizing that the Holy Spirit's power is more important than their own talents and abilities.

This planning does not replace the work of the Holy Spirit, but the Spirit can work through a well-planned service. Improvising is synonymous with irresponsibility and God wants His servants to be diligent. The Holy Spirit can inspire His servants through the process and the time given to planning (Leviticus 8, Luke 12:7-20).

Planning can make the difference in the worship ministry of many churches and can contribute significantly in the transformation of the worshipers' lives (the congregation, the Pastor and the Worship leaders).

Examples of activities or moments within a worship service: Praise, prayer, testimonies, tithes and offerings, sacraments, Bible readings, special songs, artistic moments, etc.

Lesson 5 - Congregational Worship

> Each moment of a worship service should be well used. It is for the worship of the Lord and the edifying of the congregation. Carrying it out with excellence demands putting one's heart, soul, mind and strength into the planning.

There are many ways to plan a service but it is very important to have the purpose of the service in mind. A well-planned worship service requires the following:

- The Pastor asks the Worship team to put together a worship program based on the theme of the sermon (the objective of the service).
- The musicians look for hymns and/or songs that relate to the theme.
- The Bible reading should be a passage that complements the text of the sermon.
- A special song can also add to the development of the theme.
- The introductory words of the service can emphasis the message, just as every part of the service should.

The emphasis does not have to be so very explicit, but can be mentioned in subtle ways. On the other hand, it would be a waste of time to plan a service that has no connection (explicit or implicit) with the message of the preaching. Also, it is important to vary the order of the program and be creative in order to include variety and create an environment of expectation of what God is going to do in the lives of His people.

Services for Baptism and Holy Communion

Those services that include the sacraments deserve special planning.

Baptism is an important event in the beginning of the Christian's life. When planning a baptism service, there are many details to consider. For example, we should ask, "Where will the baptism take place? How will we do it? How many will be baptized? What role will the new believers take? What will be the order of service? How can we use the baptism service to encourage others to have a personal encounter with Christ, to begin discipleship classes and be part of the family of God through baptism?

> *As Christians, we believe that God heals the sick. The Manual for the Church of the Nazarene states the following: "We believe in the Bible doctrine of divine healing and urge our people to seek to offer the prayer of faith for the healing of the sick" (Article of Faith, XIV).*

The Communion service should be celebrated frequently. The Manual of the Church of the Nazarene says that Pastors should offer Communion at least once every three months (*Manual 2009-2013, article 413.9*) although there are many churches that celebrate it one Sunday each month. Holy Communion is rich in significance and there are various ways to celebrate it. It is a sacrament that commemorates the sacrifice of our Lord Jesus (I Corinthians 11:26). However there are many teachings related to this sacrament. For example, the connection between Communion and Passover (Exodus 12); the celebration of Jesus' resurrection and the second coming (Luke 22:16); the community aspect of worship to Jesus (I Corinthians 10:16-17 or John 17:20-23); Jesus being the bread of life (John 6:53); the connection between the bread as a symbol of the body of Christ which is broken for us and the Body of Christ which is the church (Ephesians 5:25-27), among others, may be highlighted teachings to celebrate Holy Communion.

The Planning of Special Services

Special services require a different type of planning.

In special services, an endless number of significant moments can be celebrated. These events can be unforgettable moments, or if not well planned, they may be barely even noticed. Many of these occasions are great opportunities to link the congregation to the people of the community.

Testimony Services and Thanksgiving Services

A testimony of a new believer, a sanctification experience, a testimony of protection and provision of God, are as all tools that the Lord uses to impact the lives of many people. These services can serve many different purposes:

To publically glorify God for his miraculous work
To evangelize
To sanctify
To anoint and pray for the sick
To promote the ministries of evangelism and discipleship
To sense the call of God (pastors and laypersons)
To promote a new class, such as a class on personal finance or a class for parents with adolescents, etc.

Special Holidays and Celebrations

During each year, there are special moments that deserve to be celebrated, such as the anniversary of the local church, the anniversary of the Church of the Nazarene, Pastor's Day, Teacher's Day, a day of special service recognition for a servant of the Lord, church building dedication, the organization of a new church, the presentation and installation of a new pastor, a tribute to a Pastor who is retiring, among others.

Any special moment in the church or community can become a special event in the life of the congregation.

The Christian calendar is full of commemorative dates that should be celebrated, such as the following: Holy Week, Easter, Pentecost, and Christmas, among others. Also, there are special holidays such as Mother's Day, Father's Day, and Children's Day. These holidays can be celebrated in a Sunday service or at any other day and time.

These special celebrations are wonderful days to invite friends and neighbors of the community to the church.

The Christian worship service should not be a "show" to please or entertain the congregation.

What Did We Learn?

When planning a worship service to God, there should be clear objectives. Each part of the service should be planned very carefully so that it will be a transforming experience of celebration and of spiritual strengthening in the life of the congregation.

Activities

INSTRUCTIONS:

1. In today's world, believers have different versions of the Bible. Therefore, one must take care in planning the reading of the Word during the service. For example, when a congregational reading is planned, what suggestions can be given to really hear the Word of God in place of hearing many voices reading different versions or lacking coordination?

_____
_____
_____
_____

2. One moment that requires creativity is the baptism service, especially when a time is needed to change clothes after the baptisms. In general, this time is filled with an additional praise (singing) time; however, no moment of a service should be for just "filling" space. What ideas can you give for filling this moment that would be more meaningful?

_____
_____
_____
_____

3. In groups of 3 or 4, evaluate the order of worship in your church. Is there a clear objective that is accomplished during the service? Do the worship services meet the planned, specific objectives? Share with the class in a constructive way.

_____
_____
_____
_____

4. In the same groups, design an order of worship for a service that is different than the normal services you experience, but that has all the specific objectives studied in this lesson.

_____
_____
_____
_____
_____

Lesson 6

THE HOLY SPIRIT AND WORSHIP

Objectives

- To know who the Holy Spirit is and what He does.
- To understand that only the Spirit makes us true worshipers.

Main Ideas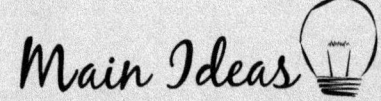

- The same Spirit that Jesus possesses lives in His children.
- The Holy Spirit allows us to love God more.
- Only by being temples of the Holy Spirit can we worship God in spirit and in truth.

Introduction

At the creation of the world that we read about in Genesis 1 and 2, we can see the Spirit of God in action. Later, in the Old Testament we find the Holy Spirit giving the message of God to the prophets. In the New Testament, the Spirit is revealed in the person of Jesus Christ, directing His life and ministry. When Jesus went to heaven, He left the Holy Spirit to inhabit the church.

Revelation: the voluntary act of God that gives knowledge to human beings and leads them to desire friendship with Him.

The Spirit is the divine agent that works in the children of God, giving them spiritual and eternal life, recreating in them the image of God that was distorted by sin, teaching them to live a life of holiness, and guiding them in the mission of reaching the lost. The Spirit reveals the Son and leads the Christian to the truth.

The Holy Spirit in the Old Testament

In the Old Testament, the Spirit anointed the leaders of the people of God.

To study more about the work of the Spirit in salvation: John 1:12,13; 3:5,6, 36 and 5:24; Ephesians 2:5,6; Titus 3:5,6; Galatians 5:25.

In the Old Testament, the Spirit was referred to as the "Spirit" (Genesis 6:3), "Spirit of God" (2 Chronicles 15:2), "Spirit of Jehovah" (Isaiah 11:12), "Breath of the Almighty" (Job 32:8) and "Spirit of the Lord" (Isaiah 61:11).

The Old Testament reveals the Holy Spirit as the dynamic presence of God in creation (Genesis 1:1,2), giving life to the first human couple and as the giver of life and breath. (Genesis 2:7, Job 33:4). Later on in the story, the ministry of the Spirit was focused on helping those who were chosen by God to give them spiritual, intellectual and physical trainings, generally for the purpose of leading the people of God.

The Holy Spirit is who gives the ability and the motivation to mankind to respond to the love of God through worship, both as individuals and in community.

To anoint someone with oil represented the presence of the Spirit in the life of a person. Among these leaders, we find priests, prophets, judges, kings and people with great talents and artistic abilities for the construction of the Temple (Exodus 31:1-6, Judges 3:10, 1 Samuel 11:6). The Spirit's mission in the Old Testament was to inspire the prophets, and through them the message was given to the kings, the nation of Israel and other nations (Micah 3:8, Ezekiel 11:5).

The prophets were the ones who announced that the Spirit of God would be poured out on the people of God. For those who lived in the days when Jesus walked on the Earth, this was accomplished at Pentecost (Joel 2:28-29, Isaiah 44:33, Isaiah 59:21, Ezekiel 39:29 and Acts 2:39). The action of the Spirit would now occur in human hearts. The Spirit would work to regenerate and sanctify (Ezekiel 37:14, 36:26,27; Jeremiah 31:33; I Corinthians 3:16; 2 Corinthians 3:3,6).

In Hebrew, the word "spirit" signifies blowing, wind, air. It is identified as the life-giving breath of God. This breath of God is what gives human's life. Without God's Spirit, we would just be inert material (Genesis 2:7; Job 33:4; Ezekiel 37:9).

The Work of the Holy Spirit in the Old Testament	
1) God anointed with the Holy Spirit those He called to a special ministry	Exodus 31:3; Judges 3:10; 1 Samuel 16:13; 1 Peter 1:10
2) The servants of God are covered with the Spirit for a time, and later on the Spirit may be taken from them.	1 Samuel 10:10; Ezekiel 2:2, 3:4; Psalm 51:13 among others.
3) The work of the Holy Spirit in the human heart was not complete until Christ made the purification of hearts possible by His death on the cross. For this reason, the Old Testament says that the Spirit rested on a person, but it does not say the Spirit was "in" a person.	Numbers 11:25; Judges 3:10, 11:29; 1 Corinthians 12:13.

The Holy Spirit Beginning at Pentecost

The Holy Spirit was poured out on the church and guides ministry.

Pentecost was more than just the beginning of the Christian era. It marked the beginning of a new time when God began to work in the hearts of His servants in a different and deep way. It was not until Pentecost that God completed His promise to pour His Spirit on all mankind (Acts 2:17). God put His Spirit in both men and women (John 16:7; 14:16-17). Before Pentecost, this was not possible since Christ had not died and risen again. His death and resurrection made possible the purification of sins in the lives of His disciples.

In the New Testament, all the ministry of the Spirit is based on the work of Jesus Christ. The object of the ministry of the Holy Spirit is to bring glory to Jesus (John 16:13-14). Without the action of the Holy Spirit, no one can receive the fullness of Christ. It is for this reason that in the rest of the books

Jesus uses the metaphor of the wind to illustrate the life giving work of the Spirit in the hearts of His followers (John 3:8; 29:22 and Habakkuk 2:2).

Lesson 6 - The Holy Spirit and Worship

of the New Testament, the Holy Spirit is referred to as "Spirit of Jesus" (Acts 16:7), "Spirit of Christ" (Romans 8:9), and "Spirit of the Son" (Galatians 6:4). All these terms refer to the same Spirit, namely, the third person of the Trinity as explained by Rene Pache: "...for the Scriptures, the Holy Spirit, the Spirit of God and the Spirit of Christ are all one unique Person" (17).

Believers should be careful to not "lie to the Spirit" (Acts 5:3), "tempt the Spirit" (Acts 5:9), "resist the Spirit" (Acts 7:51), "grieve the Spirit" (Ephesians 4:30), "insult" the Spirit (Hebrews 10:29) or blaspheme against the Holy Spirit" (Matthew 12:31).

What the Holy Spirit Is and What He Does

The Holy Spirit acts to guide the children of God to His heart.

Jesus announced that He had the power to send the Holy Spirit to live inside the hearts of men and women who believed in Him (John 16:7; 14:16-17).

When the Holy Spirit inhabits the children of God (1 John 2:2), the Father and the Son are present also (1 John 3:24). The Holy Spirit inhabits Christ's disciples and sustains them (John 4:14; 14:17).

What the Holy Spirit Is	What the Holy Spirit Does
The Holy Spirit is a divine person, as is the Father and the Son.	Convinces the sinner of sin, righteousness and judgment so that he or she can come to salvation.
He is the "seal" that distinguishes the children of God (Ephesians 1:33, 4:30 and 2 Corinthians 1:22).	Lives inside true believers from the moment that they accept Christ as Savior and Lord and they become the temple of the Holy Spirit (Romans 8:9,11; 1 Corinthians 3:16,17; 6:19; 2 Corinthians 13:5, 6:16).
He is the water of life that was promised by Jesus (John 6:35; 7:38,39).	The Spirit makes it possible for believers to be children of God. He is the one who gives new life to the believer, baptizes the believer and "adopts" the believer into the family of God (Romans 8:15).
Characteristics and attributes of the Holy Spirit: "goodness" (Nehemiah 9:20), "wisdom," "counsel," "knowledge" (Isaiah 11:2), "holiness" (Psalm 51:13), "grace and supplication"(Zechariah 12:10), and the "fear of the Lord" (Isaiah 11:2).	Communicates with the spirit of the Christian (John 14:17-20).
The Holy Spirit is a gift from God to His children (Romans 6:23).	Imparts the life of Christ (John 4:14; 6:35; 10:10; Romans 8:2; John 6:63).

To study more about the filling of the Spirit in the New Testament Church:
In leaders:
Hebrews 8:4; 11:24; 13:9
In elders: Acts 6:3; 7:55
In discipleship groups: Acts 2:4
In large groups: Acts 4:4.

The Filling of the Spirit

In the early days of the church, being filled with the Holy Spirit was not an option; it was a requirement (Hebrews 12:4 and Ephesians 4:13). To be filled with the Spirit was the same as being "full of grace" as Jesus was. Without the Spirit, the believer could be filled with perverse qualities such as the following: anger (Acts 19:28; Luke 4:28), rage (Luke 6:11) or jealousy (Acts 5:17, 13:45) among others.

Paul affirms that perversions come from Satan and they cannot remain in the heart that is full of the Spirit of God (Acts 5:3, 13:9). A heart that is not full of the Spirit lives inclined to do evil.

Paul encouraged the Corinthians to be filled with the Holy Spirit. He affirms that although they had been baptized and had been born of the Spirit, they were still like children, unable to assimilate and apply the deeper spiritual things (I Corinthians 1:13; 6:9; and 3:1-3).

The Galatians were also in danger of leaving the true gospel behind and throwing away the work of Paul all because they were not filled with the Spirit (Galatians 1:13; 6:9; and 3:1-3).

Paul teaches the church of Ephesus that God desires that all believers, no matter the time period they live in, be filled with the Holy Spirit (Ephesians 5:18). God always wants us to be filled more and more with the Spirit. As James writes in chapter 4, verse 5: "Or do you think Scripture says without reason that he jealously longs for the spirit he has caused to dwell in us?" It is the same as a parent whose deepest desire is for his children to be filled with good health and strength.

> Some passages that affirm that God sanctifies the believer in a particular moment so they are filled with the Holy Spirit are these: Romans 15:16; 1 Corinthians 6:11; 2 Thessalonians 2:13; and 1 Peter 1:2.

How does one receive the Spirit?

Every grace that God gives requires an open heart. In order that the Holy Spirit can fill a human heart, certain conditions of receptivity must exist:

1. Confession of all known sin. This is necessary since sin impedes the Spirit from filling the heart.

2. A deep desire to receive the fullness of the Spirit. Paul uses the metaphor of water and thirst to illustrate that the Spirit will not deny filling the heart that so earnestly desires it.

3. Complete abandon to the hands of God. In this act of surrender, God accepts us as an offering and receives us just as we are. God wants our permission to enter every part of our being to transform and purify us. He does not wait for us to remove the sin before He enters; instead, he enters to free us from sin (Philippians 2:13).

> To be filled with the Spirit does not imply that the believer has more of the Holy Spirit. On the contrary, it means that God has more of the Christian, who having given up putting his or her selfish desires first, now puts himself or herself completely at the feet of God so that God uses the believer's life according to His purposes.

> *"Let anyone who is thirsty come to me and drink. Whoever believes in me, as Scripture has said, rivers of living water will flow from within them."*
> *John 7:37-38.*

4. The fullness of the Spirit is received by faith. It is essential to believe that God will accomplish His promise and fill all of our being (John 4:14; 7:37-39). This faith should be placed in Jesus Christ, not in other people or in ourselves. We must believe that He will be present with us each day through His Spirit.

5. In an instant (Acts 2:4; 4:31; 9:17). "We believe that there is a marked distinction between a pure heart and a mature character. The former is obtained in an instant, the result of entire sanctification; the latter is the result of growth in grace.

We believe that the grace of entire sanctification includes the divine impulse to grow in grace as a Christlike disciple. However, this impulse must be consciously nurtured, and careful attention given to the requisites and processes of spiritual development and improvement in Christlikeness of character and personality. Without such purposeful endeavor, one's witness may be impaired and the grace itself frustrated and ultimately lost" (Church of the Nazarene Manual, Articles of Faith, X, 14).

Results of the Filling of the Spirit	
A Purity Within	Matthew 3:11,12; Luke 3:16,17; John 7:39; 15:3; 16:7; 17:7; 1 Corinthians 3:13-15; Ephesians 5:26
Perfection of Love	1 Corinthians 13
Fruit of the Spirit	Galatians 5:16,17
Constant Growth	Romans 8:29; Ephesians 4:13, 3:19; John 14:26, 7:38-39; 2 Timothy 1:7
Power to do the Work of Ministry	Acts 1:29; 2:41; 7:55-56; 13:2-4; 16:6-8

Worshiping God in Spirit and truth is to experience an encounter with the Spirit of the Living God in daily life.

From the moment of the filling of the Spirit, the believer experiences progressive victory over sin since he or she has been made free from the law of sin and death (Romans 8:2; 2 Corinthians 3:17).

The Spirit cleanses from all impurity and produces divine fruit (Galatians 5:22). This inner purification eliminates everything that impedes the perfect communion with God.

But believers can only reach the perfect likeness of Christ in glory (1 John 3:2), which reveals that there is more to receive from the Spirit of God after our physical deaths.

Through encounters with God, either privately or publically, the Holy Spirit has the opportunity to complete His work in our lives. At the same time, the Spirit teaches us to worship God with all our heart, all our mind, and with all our strength, which is to say with a sincere heart whose love for God is whole and true.

What Did We Learn?

The Holy Spirit trains Christians to worship. The Holy Spirit is who trains and motivates the believer to respond to the love of God through individual as well as community worship.

Activities

Time 20'

INSTRUCTIONS:

1. What is the role of the Holy Spirit in worship?
   _____
   _____
   _____

2. Explain why the worshiper needs to be filled with the Holy Spirit.
   _____
   _____
   _____

3. Which of the ministries that the Holy Spirit does has special significance to you and your spiritual growth?
   _____
   _____
   _____

4. In groups of three or four students, respond to this question: How has your private and your community worship experiences helped you to love God even more?
   _____
   _____
   _____

5. Complete the following table comparing aspects of your life before and after becoming a Christian, and then with your life as a Spirit-filled Christian. These aspects of your life may be ways in which you think, talk or act.

My life without Christ	My life before being Spirit-filled	My Spirit-filled life

Lesson 7

STEWARDSHIP AS AN ACT OF WORSHIP

Objectives

- Define "stewardship"
- Understand stewardship as an act of worship.
- Appreciate the various dimensions of Christian stewardship.

Main Ideas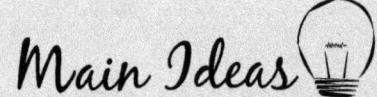

- A steward is an administrator of another person's goods.
- Christian stewardship begins with recognizing that God is the owner of all we are and all we have.
- A faithful steward offers his or her life and possessions to the service of Jesus Christ.

Introduction

Stewardship is the translation of the Greek word *"oikonomia"*, which is made up of two words: *"oiko"* which means house and *"nomos"* which means law. Therefore, the word stewardship refers to the managing of a home and the affairs associated with it.

Steward: *A person whose responsibility is to administrate the home and the possessions of another.*

In the Gospels, an *"oikonomia"* or steward is a slave or servant who is trusted by the homeowner to care for the management of the house. "Who then is the faithful and wise manager, whom the master puts in charge of his servants to give them their food allowance at the proper time?" (Luke 12:42). The term takes on spiritual meaning when Jesus uses it as a spiritual metaphor describing the way a person manages his or her own life before God.

In the Pauline epistles, *"oikonomia"* is used by Paul to define his commission to preach the Gospel (I Corinthians 9:17). He speaks of himself as a steward of the grace of God (Ephesians 3:2) and of the mysteries of God (I Corinthians 4:1).

One of the responsibilities that God gave to the church leaders was to teach the believers to recognize God as the Creator and Redeemer of their entire lives. This realization should lead to a holy care of all that God has placed in their hands. Stewardship is the final result of the awareness of the reality that all that we are and have has been given to us by a generous God. We must wisely administrate what God has given us and share it with generosity.

The Meaning of Stewardship

In this section we will learn three principles of stewardship.

There are three basic principles included in the concept of stewardship. First of all, the term implies the existence of an owner. Jesus reminded his disciples many times that God is not only the creator and sustainer, but also the owner of all that exists. Centuries before, the Psalmist said, "The earth is the LORD'S, and everything in it, the world, and all who live in it" (Psalm 24:1). The apostles also emphasized that everything belonged to God. Acts 4:32 says, "No one claimed that any of their possessions was their own, but they shared everything they had." Everything in this life is a gift from God. He is the creator and provider of all that mankind possesses.

Secondly, if one understands that God is the owner of everything, then this naturally lead to the fact that God has the right to designate people to be His administrators or stewards. The third principle is the need for the steward to give an account to the Creator for the use of all that he has been entrusted with.

Finally, to be a steward means having received a certain amount of trust from the owner that the person will carefully manage what has been given. For a Christian, stewardship means that everything we have has been received from God to manage well so that one day we may give an account of all we have received.

The majority of people think that stewardship has to do with money and possessions. It is obvious that we have a responsibility not only before God, but also to our neighbors for the manner in which we manage God's resources. Most people would agree that one can judge the character of a person by how he or she uses possessions, and especially in the way money is spent.

But what is money? There is no doubt that money is a symbol of something else. It is a symbol of work. The major part of the money that circulates is from the fact that work has been done and so payment must be made. These symbols of human labor are recognized in the workplace and businesses. Then these symbols are traded for other symbols of work, such as bread. But, what is bread? It is a symbol of the work of another man, perhaps a farmer or a baker. We need to think about this and ask ourselves, "What is work?" Labor takes time. So in this way, we can say that work is time.

When we speak of a steward of money, then we are really speaking of a steward of time. For believers to be good stewards, they must consecrate their possessions, their time and their lives to God. This is the way that Jesus teaches us to have a victorious life.

Stewardship of Time

How should a Christian manage time?

When believers discover that their time and talents are on loan from God, this inevitably brings up a question: What is the best way for me to use my time for the benefit of the work of God in the world?

For Christians, stewardship means that all that we have is a gift from God to be managed correctly. One day we will have to give an account of how we administrated what we received.

Everyone can and should serve in the church. Our best gift to God is our own life.

Lesson 7 - Stewardship as an Act of Worship

Luis thinks that if someone has few worldly possessions then being a good steward is not a problem. He does not have many possessions, and the way in which he uses the small amount he has is not a problem for him. The little he makes he rapidly uses for the basic necessities of his family and there is little left to share with others or with the church. However, Luis is mistaken in the way he understands the concept of stewardship.

Luis has the same opportunity to give as others since he has the same amount of time each day as everyone else, whether they are rich or poor. God has given us life and that life is made up of time. It is not only the eight work hours of the day that have worth. All the rest of the day has been given to us by God to manage.

We should learn to measure time wisely, giving it its proper worth, remembering that once it is gone there is no way to get it back.

There are those who think of stewardship in terms of the number of hours dedicated to the work of the church, the amount of time given to social activities, work, family, etc. This is important, without a doubt, but the stewardship of time involves more than just giving a part of "our" time to God. Stewardship of time should be measured not only in the length of time, but also in the depth of time. That is to say, time should be measured not by quantity, but by quality. The use of time should be based on correct priorities.

For example, it is not correct to dedicate so much time to the work of God that we neglect our families and our health. Neither is it correct to dedicate so much time to recreation that we do not take care of our home. And it is not right to spend so much time at work to earn more money to buy more things that are non-essentials, while giving so little time in the service of God.

So, it is very important to find an adequate balance in time management so that appropriate attention is given to all the responsibilities according to the priorities that God has established. This time distribution has to be made in accordance with the different life stages we encounter as humans.

The truth is that the important thing to God is not how long we live, but how we spend the time while we are alive. We should learn to measure the time according to the value it has, knowing that once it is gone there is no way to get it back. Many things in which Christians invest so much time, for example watching television, playing video games, and other things, are useless activities. They do not provide for your health, they do not strengthen relationships, they do not contribute financially for the family, nor do they strengthen relationships. These things are not a good way to serve God or to share His love with others.

Christians need to be more responsible in the use of their time, using it to glorify God.

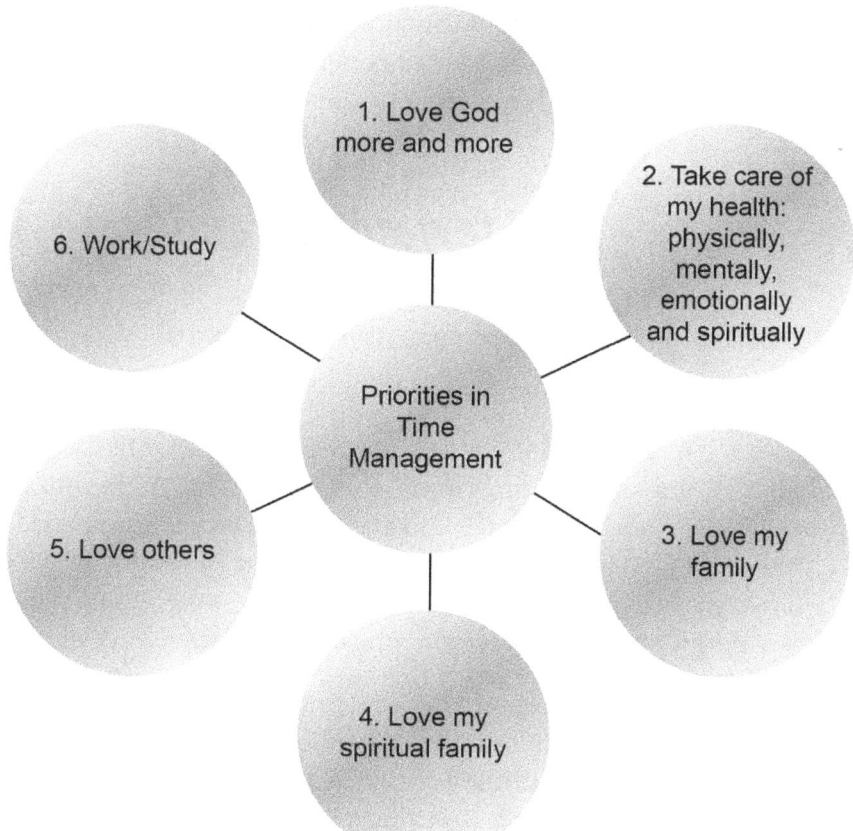

Stewardship of Talents

Everyone has unique talents given by God to serve others.

Some people think that the only ones who have the responsibility to serve in the church are those who have special talents or gifts. People tend to admire and almost "envy" those who have musical, preaching or leadership gifts. But it is not correct to think that certain skills are more important than others. To God, there are not people with special talents and people that are "common." Everyone is blessed with valid qualities to serve God and others.

Every Christian has abilities given to them by God to complete a special and unique purpose in the kingdom.

Everyone can and should serve in the church. Our biggest talent is our life. For example, everyone has learned important lessons from their own life experiences, from their daily walk with Christ, and from their teachers and pastors at church, and we can offer all this to God and use it to serve others. Even the most difficult trials or most painful experiences can be transformed into a tool of blessing that can help others passing through similar experiences.

Lesson 7 - Stewardship as an Act of Worship

Each Christian has unique abilities that have been given by God to complete a special purpose in the Kingdom. God desires us to be good stewards of our gifts and skills so we can complete His will and purpose. No one can take your place in this assignment. God wants us to give our lives to bless others.

Stewardship and Possessions

In this section, we will see the importance of honesty in stewardship.

To study more about the teachings of Jesus concerning the use of money, refer to these Scriptures:
Matthew 6:24
Mark 12:41-43
Mark 12:16
Luke 12:59
Luke 21:2
John 6:1-13

The Lord often spoke about possessions and money. In Matthew 6:24, Jesus taught that the love of money and riches is not compatible with the Christian life. He knew that money and possessions represent our strength, energy, time and talent and that when we share a part of what we have earned in our work, we are giving a part of ourselves. On the other hand, when we are selfish with our possessions, we are refusing to give of ourselves.

In our society, money represents power, prestige and security. It is so easy for money and possessions to become the center of our love and attention. An incorrect attitude concerning money can very easily transform into a spiritual sickness of the heart.

The material and spiritual are inseparable in our lives. We are all humans, made of skin and bones, but we are also spiritual beings. Each one of these areas is related to and affects the others. Jesus wants to be the Lord of our entire lives, including our money, possessions, physical bodies, minds and spirits. It is for this reason that the Lord is so interested in the way we make, use and share our money.

God requires that all our material possessions be placed under His sovereignty. This means that God can use or ask for any possession at any moment to be used in His work.

God requires that all our material possessions be under His authority. This means that God can ask for or use whatever possession at whatever moment for use in His Kingdom. Honesty is an important quality in good stewardship. If we say that God is our Lord but we do not give one hundred percent of who we are and what we have, then we are lying. The quality of our spiritual lives will depend on the way in which we worship God will our entire beings, being faithful in the administration of our material resources.

Tithing as an Essential Act of Stewardship

Now we will understand the meaning of tithing as an act of faithfulness.

The tithe means giving to God ten percent of all the material gains that a Christian has received as a fruit of his or her labor, inheritance or investment. The first time that tithing is mentioned in the Bible is in the

School of Leadership - Worship as a Lifestyle

history of Abraham who gave his tithe to the priest Melchizedek (Genesis 14:17-20). A thankful heart motivated Jacob when he gave a tithe of his goods (Genesis 28:20-22).

Later on in the history of Israel, the tithe was established as a thanks offering to God for the many blessings received. It was not offered as an obligation, but was freely given. However, the tithe was not the only thing given to God by the Jews. They offered the first sheep or goats of their flocks and the first fruits of their harvests. These goods were taken to the Temple and given to the priests.

The members of the Christian churches have continued the practice of tithing until today and in this way everyone who is part of God's family has the privilege of contributing in the extension of the reign of God on the Earth.

Those of us who are part of God's family have the privilege of contributing with our money and our possessions to extend the reign of God on Earth.

What Did We Learn?

All Christians should learn to be faithful stewards of their time, abilities and possessions. Knowing Christ as Lord implies recognizing God as the owner of our entire life. We should demonstrate this by the way we manage our lives, giving glory and worship to God with all that we are and all that we have.

Activities

Time 20'

INSTRUCTIONS:

1. Write your own definition of stewardship.
   _____
   _____
   _____
   _____

2. Mention three qualities of good stewards.
   _____
   _____
   _____

3. What changes do you need to make in your life starting now in order to be a better steward?
   _____
   _____
   _____
   _____

4. Mention the areas of your life where you are responsible to faithfully administrate what God has given to you.
   _____
   _____
   _____
   _____

5. In groups of three or four, explain the relationship between stewardship and worship.
   _____
   _____
   _____
   _____
   _____
   _____

Lesson 8

CULTURAL FUNDAMENTALS OF WORSHIP

Objectives

- To study the cultural fundamentals of worship.
- To analyze some characteristics of postmodernism.
- To understand the relationship between culture and worship.

Main Ideas

- Worship is a powerful tool that transforms culture because of its deep meaning and spiritual principles.
- Jesus challenged the cultural trends of His community.
- The church is called to be an agent of change and transformation.

Introduction

Church history reveals that there are a variety of ways in which people express their faith. This is because the way worship is expressed is conditioned by the historical situation and the cultural context of the believer. Each culture has adopted its own way to worship based on particular forms and styles. It is an error to think that a form of liturgical expression will look the same in all socio-cultural contexts. The church needs to remember as it does mission work, that the daily experiences and the psychosocial conditions of the culture deeply influence the way in which the members understand and express faith.

When Christ, the divine Son of God, became human, he was born into a Jewish nuclear family and adapted to the culture. The church as the body of Christ works in different cultures, and in so doing lives out the mission of Christ and continues the mission on Earth. That is to say, the church is called to be the agent of change and transformation in the community where it finds itself, communicating the good news following the style of the given culture. This is what is called "contextualization."

Culture and Its Forms

Culture is a set of patterns that are common to a group of people that organize human life and society.

All cultures have accepted and unaccepted forms of conduct.

Culture describes the identity of a group of people.

Culture is a set of standards common to a group of people. These standards organize human life and society and are considered "normal" for the group. For example, it is normal in some cultures to greet one another with a kiss, while in other cultures people greet with a handshake or bow. These specific behaviors are called norms, and they provide the evaluation criteria to know if conduct is normal or abnormal. An unexpected behavior outside of the norm causes problems in relationships and reduces trust between people.

People in a particular culture tend to close themselves off to conducts or behaviors that seem new because they threaten their way of life and security. This is easily seen when a group of people worship God in a way that is normal and comfortable to them, but perhaps shocking and disrespectful to others.

Culture also describes the roles that people play. For example, what is it that constitutes expected behavior for men and women? In a society, there may be many different roles. When a society organizes itself in a way that gives one group of individuals or families certain benefits above others, concepts of justice and equality can be abandoned. Just as Jesus denounced social classes and politics of oppression, the church should communicate and promote God's justice.

How Should the Church Live Within the Culture?

The church is called to be incarnate in the culture, transforming it with the love of God.

Jesus accepted some cultural elements of the day, but rejected those that were in conflict with the Kingdom of God. The Apostle Paul declares that Christ did not think of Himself, but took on the nature of a servant and in this way humbled himself, being obedient even to death on the cross (Philippians 2:7,8). What does this mean for us? It means that we have been placed in this world to have an incarnational ministry and to enter into the culture to continue Jesus' ministry. Christians are exposed to the same temptations as others, experiencing the strengths and weaknesses of the culture in which we live, but enjoying the benefits that come from being in communion with Christ, which gives the strength to resist the power of evil.

The term "acculturation" refers to the process that occurs when a person from one culture makes adjustments in order to adapt to a new cultural influence. The adaptation that occurs when learning to use new technology like a new cell phone is an example of acculturation.

When Christians isolate themselves from society, they are not in a position to help others find freedom (John 8:31-32). God's plan is not for Christians to remove themselves from the world, but to send themselves into the world to reveal the holiness of God so the world will know Him (John 17:14-18). The goal of every Christian is to show how the truth and love of God can transform a society of oppression and injustice. Societies are transformed when individuals are transformed by the power of God.

What are Cultural Values?

The church should live according to the values of the Kingdom of God.

The values of a culture are the positive and worthy goals that motivate people's conduct. Shared values help the group to enter into a dialogue when there are problems, and then find solutions together. The concept of happiness is based on living according to the values that the society imposes.

Lesson 8 - Cultural Fundamentals of Worship

Cultural values are reflected in one's understanding of the gospel and worship. At the same time, the gospel is a powerful tool that can transform culture since it proposes a "countercultural" lifestyle. This means that the gospel makes people question all cultural aspects that are contrary to the gospel of Jesus Christ.

Christians should check the culture against the values of the Kingdom of God and in that way identify the sinful aspects of the culture. For example, in capitalist countries, there exists the tendency to accumulate goods, but Jesus taught that we should not be slaves to riches, but instead share what we have willingly with others as the early church did. "All the believers were together and had everything in common. They sold property and possessions to give to anyone who had need" (Acts 2:44-45).

In its missionary work, the church should promote the values of the Kingdom of God, both in the lifestyle of the congregation and in the message of the church. Some of these values include love, justice, peace, and participating in the process of restoration of human beings to the image and likeness of God (Ephesians 4:11-15).

Examples of categories that make cultural standards evident:
- Couple and family roles
- Sex, marriage and family
- Ways to make a living
- Economic system
- Language
- Communication
- Politics
- National celebrations
- Artistic expression
- Illness and healing
- Religious beliefs: behaviors and symbolism
- Symbols of wealth and power

Values can be placed in categories. Here is an example.

Personal Values (values that have to do with one's being)	Relational Values (values that allow people to live in harmony together)
Love	Honesty
Self-esteem	Family
Health	Kindness
Happiness	Impartiality
Freedom	Creativity
Wisdom	Loyalty
Companionship	Flexibility
Reaching goals	Stability
Peace	Tolerance
Service	Being autonomous
	Forgiveness
	Competence
	Understanding
	Initiative
	Reason

What is the Relationship Between the Culture and the Church Service?

In the church service, worship can be expressed in different cultural ways.

There are at least four ways that a Christian worship service can be culturally dynamic. First, worship is transcultural. There are aspects of worship that are evident in all cultures. Some of these are baptism, Holy Communion, the preaching of the Word, the reading of the Word, songs, prayers and the fact that the people of God are to reach the world through mission. These aspects form the basis for a common culture sometimes called the "gospel culture" that unites all Christians. Secondly, the worship service is contextual because in each culture the act of worship has its own unique expression, which gives a rich diversity in worship.

Counterculture is the third aspect. We recognize that in every culture there are elements that are sinful, dehumanizing, and that contradict the values and principles of the Gospel. Christian faith and worship challenges all types of oppression, inequality and injustice wherever they exist. The fourth element is intercultural. We recognize that Christians from various cultures share a similar worship foundation and this strengthens their unity before Christ. Intercultural expression can enrich the worship of any local church.

Christian values help us to understand the "language" of our hearts. It is important to take into account that God understands our culture, He speaks to us in our own language and He rejoices in the ways we prefer to worship Him.

Culture and its Affect on Worship Ministers

The affects of the postmodern culture on worship ministers.

When one examines the world's culture and how it influences those who lead Christian worship, one can see a strong temptation toward selfishness and self-centeredness. When this is prevalent in the culture, it can lead to elevating the singer or leader to be the most important part of the worship service. Sometimes there may be music in the church service, but not worship.

It is important that those who direct the church worship understand that the Christian leader is first and foremost a minister and secondly a musician, not the reverse. That is to say that the musicians serve both God and the congregation accompanied by the music, which is the communication of the redeemed people of God to their Father. The music can provide an environment that makes it easier for the believers to express their worship to God. But the worship is not in the music. The music, in and of itself, is not equal to worship, nor is it the only valid way to worship God.

What does the verb "minister" mean? To give support to someone in something. It is a synonym to the word assist, help and support.

Lesson 8 - Cultural Fundamentals of Worship

A worshiper should be a minister that has his or her eyes fixed on Jesus and is willing to serve the congregation. Ministry should include preparation, training, and above all, the calling of the Lord.

The people that lead worship should have gifts for their service, be called by God and be trained for their ministry. (1 Chronicles 25:1-8, Ephesians 4:11).

It is just this lack of understanding that leads musicians to act as "artists" or to feel responsible to give a good "show." It is sad to see how in some churches as the last song is sung, the musicians leave the worship service and do not participate in the rest of the service. It is also sad when the musicians do not attend Sunday School classes, are not involved in evangelism or discipleship or any other ministry. These behaviors reveal that the musicians do not see themselves as ministers.

The worship ministers should be very clear about their priorities:

- To please God in spirit and in truth, and to be a genuine worshiper with correct attitudes and motives.
- To be sensitive to the direction of the Holy Spirit and be submissive to the leadership of the church.
- To direct in a way that exalts Christ, emphasizing the Person of Christ, being humble and submissive to the Lordship of Jesus.
- To make ministering to the congregation the main objective and to do this according to the congregation's needs.

A Church that Transforms the Culture

A true church transforms its context.

John and Charles Wesley were born during a time of terrible immorality and social corruption in England in the 18th century. Inspired by the Holy Spirit, they developed an evangelism and discipleship strategy that changed the history of England. They wanted to respond to the sinful issues that confronted the society such as slavery, alcoholism, exploitation in the workplace and moral degradation, among others.

For John Wesley, worship did not end with the liturgy, but instead held a prominent place in the mission. The small group strategy that Wesley implemented provided the environment for spiritual fellowship and restoration. The members won the victory over sin, became productive human beings and contributed to the restoration of the poor and oppressed.

Each congregation has the freedom to develop their worship services in the way they consider best for the people in their culture. There are many ways to worship God.

What can the church do when facing cultural challenges? In the letter to the Romans the Apostle Paul says: " Do not conform to the pattern of this world, but be transformed by the renewing of your mind. Then you will be able to test and approve what God's will is—his good, pleasing and perfect will" (Romans 12:2).

The emphasis in this passage is to be transformed and not be conformed. Christians should not take on the sinful aspects of the culture around them, but instead be a model of holy living.

The church is a new nation, a new society with principles and values, and a new culture united around the Lordship of Christ. It does not simply promote a way of thinking or believing, but also promotes a new way to be in the world. The church is called to influence and transform society where it lives and worships. The church has a special mission: "Go and make disciples of all nations" which includes teaching the people of the world to live like Christ.

What Did We Learn?

Worship is expressed in different ways depending on your culture, although there are some worship characteristics that all Christians share. This can be called the "gospel culture." The church of Christ has been called to be Jesus in the nations and to teach the people of the world to live according to the principles and values of the Kingdom of God.

Activities

Time 20'

INSTRUCTIONS:

1. Define the word "culture" in your own words.
   _____
   _____
   _____
   _____

2. Identify some of the personal values and relational values in your culture.
   _____
   _____
   _____
   _____
   _____

3. Mention three or four sinful aspects of the culture in your context.
   _____
   _____
   _____
   _____

4. In pairs, respond to the following questions:

   a) Up to what point is the church committed to the transformation of society?
   _____
   _____

   b) What does it mean to be a true worshiper in a culture such as ours?
   _____
   _____
   _____
   _____

Final evaluation

Time 15'

COURSE: WORSHIP AS A LIFESTYLE

Name of Student: _____
Church or Study Center: _____
District: _____
Professor / Course: _____
Date of this evaluation: _____

1. Explain in your own words what it means to live a lifestyle of worship.

_____
_____
_____
_____

2. Mention a topic or lesson of the course that was new and helpful for you. Explain why.

_____
_____
_____
_____

3. Explain how this course helped you become a better worshiper.

_____
_____
_____
_____

4. What did you learn in the ministerial practice sections of the course?

_____
_____
_____
_____

5. In your opinion, how could this course be improved?

_____
_____
_____
_____

Bibliography

Books:

Guang Tapia, Alberto. *Hacia pastoral Paulina: Conferencia a la iglesia de Corinto.* Tesis de Licenciatura en Teología. San José, Costa Rica. Seminario Bíblico Latinoamericano: Publicaciones INDEF, 1975.

Gruden, Waine. *Teología Sistemática (Tomo I).* Miami, Florida: Editorial Vida, 2007.

Laporta, Josep. *La adoración a Dios desde una perspectiva bíblica y cúltica.* Asociación de Ministros del Evangelio de Catalunya, 2005.

Ridderbos Herman. *El pensamiento del apostol Pablo. Teologia del Nuevo Testamento.* Buenos Aires, Argentina: Ediciones Certeza, 1979

Overman J. *El cambio de una sociedad comienza con un cambio a los cristianos.* EE.UU: The Biblie Advocate Pres Grant., s.f.

Paché, René. *La persona y la obra del Espíritu Santo.* Barcelona:Clie, 1982.

Sorge, Bob. *Exploración de la adoración.* Deerfield, Florida, EE.UU: Editorial Vida, 1987.

Taylor, R.S. Grider J.K. y Taylor W.H. *Diccionario Teológico Beacon.* Kansas City: C.N.P, 1995.

Turnbull, Rodolfo G. (Ed) *Diccionario de Teología Practica Culto.* Worchip, E.U: Subcomisión Literatura Cristiana, 1977.

Vine W.E. *Diccionario expositivo de palabras de Antiguo y Nuevo Testamento exhaustivo de Vine.* Nasville, Tennesse, Grupo Nelson, 2007.

Wiersbe, Warren. *Real Worship.* Michigan: Baker Books, 2000.

Warren, Rick. *The Purpose Driven Life.* Michigan: Zondervan, 2007.

Periodicals:

Heraldo de Santidad. Arreola Freddy. *Adorad a Dios en la hermosura de su santidad.* En Volumen 55, Número 3, 2001, pp.20-21. Nazarene Publishing House, Kansas City, Missouri.

Heraldo de Santidad. Cuxum, Rony. *La opinión de un nazareno sobre la adoración.* En Volumen 55, Número 3, 2001, pp. 12-13. Nazarene Publishing House, Kansas City, Missouri.

Web Pages:

Carlos Alberto. *La adoración, un estilo de vida.* En Blog con propósito: Jazon. Recuperado en Marzo 2010 en http://carlosalbertopaz.jazon.info/

Warren, R. (). *La adoración como estilo de vida.* Publicado en revista Enfoque. Numero 29.

Recuperado el 5 de marzo 2009 en http//www.webcristiano.net/home/index.asp

Sherman Daniel. *La adoración a Dios.* Recuperado en Abril 2010 en http://www.losnavegantes.net

Stauffer S.Anita. (Ed) (1996). *Declaración de Nairobi sobre adoración y cultura en adoración cristiana:* Unidad dentro de la diversidad cristiana. Minneapolis, E.U: Augsburgo Fosrtres, Federación Mundial Luterana. Recuperado en Febrero 2010 en http://www.worship.ca/docs/lwf_ns.html

www.ingramcontent.com/pod-product-compliance
Lightning Source LLC
Chambersburg PA
CBHW080942040426
42444CB00015B/3408